THE GOD OF THE SECOND CHANCE

THE GOD
OF THE
SECOND
ChANCE

Greg Laurie

TYNDALE HOUSE PUBLISHERS, INC., WHEATON, ILLINOIS

Visit Tyndale's exciting Web site at www.tyndale.com

The God of the Second Chance

Copyright © 2002 by Greg Laurie. All rights reserved.

Cover photograph copyright © 2002 by Jon Riley/Getty Images. All rights reserved.

Designed by Jenny Swanson.

Published in 1997 as *The God of the Second Chance* by Word Publishing.

Library of Congress Cataloging-in-Publication Data

Laurie, Greg.
    The God of the second chance : experiencing forgiveness / Greg Laurie.
    p. cm.
Originally published: Dallas : Word Pub., c1997.
Includes bibliographical references.
ISBN 0-8423-5582-0 (pbk.)
1. Forgiveness—Religious aspects—Christianity.   2. Forgiveness of sin.   3. Guilt—Religious aspects—Christianity.   4. Christian life.   I. Title.
BV4647.F55 L38 2002
234'.5—dc21   2001006273

Printed in the United States of America

07   06   05   04   03   02
7   8   6   5   4   3   2   1

Dedication

THIS BOOK IS DEDICATED to my two sons, Christopher and Jonathan Laurie. May they always walk daily with the God of second chances and find His wonderful purpose for their lives.

IT IS ALSO DEDICATED to the memory of my father, Oscar Laurie, a man who was given a second chance in life and used it wisely. His life was an inspiration to me.

contents

preface

I HEARD A STORY about a man whose name was inadvertently printed in the obituary column of his local newspaper. It may have been the result of a prank or just an accident. But one day this guy woke up and read his own obituary in the paper. You can imagine how that could ruin your day. There he was, minding his own business, drinking his coffee and munching on his morning toast. He opened the newspaper and, lo and behold, he was listed as now deceased.

Not amused, the man got into his car, drove down to the newspaper office, and demanded to see the editor.

"I am outraged," the man said. "You printed my name in the obituary column. As you can see, I am obviously alive and well. This is going to be a cause of great embarrassment for me. I will probably even lose business."

"Sir, I'm sorry," said the editor. "It was an error, but there is nothing I can do."

Naturally that explanation did not appease the victim. He continued to rant and rave and even threatened to sue the paper.

Finally the editor said, "Cheer up, buddy. Tomorrow I'll put your name in the birth column and give you a fresh start."

Wouldn't it be great if it were that easy? Wouldn't it be nice to just start all over again? When you examine your life and the mistakes you've made, have you ever thought, *I wish I could start fresh, knowing what I know now?* Well, for all practical purposes, you can. The good news is there is a God who can be known, a God who you might say specializes in giving second chances—not the phony kind that the newspaper editor was willing to provide, but a real second chance, a genuine fresh start.

Why is this important? Because every one of us will, at some time or another, need a second chance. Second chances aren't just for non-Christians. Believers need them at times, too. There's a familiar verse in 1 John 1:9: "If we confess our sins, He is faithful and just to forgive us our sins and to cleanse us from all unrighteousness." Did you know that verse was actually directed toward believers? Yes, God knew that we would all fall short of perfection at one time or another. That makes the promise of forgiveness all the more significant.

No matter how many times we hear that message, though, some people inevitably feel left out. They think they have gone too far—committed some unpardonable sin, crossed God one time too often. Have you ever felt that way? Have you ever lost hope for a second chance? Perhaps you feel you've blown it in your walk with God. You've made so many wrong choices that you don't see how God could ever want to take you back. The purpose of this book is to show you there really is such a thing as a second chance—for everyone—no matter who you are or what you've done. Even for those who have failed miserably, God gives us the opportunity to put it behind us. And He can dramatically turn our lives around. Through insights fresh from the pages of God's inspired Word, this book is designed to show how we can stay spiritually strong in the days ahead, especially in times of adversity.

Maybe you've felt God calling you to do something in your life, and you've repeatedly ignored that call. You may feel comfortable with the way things are going, but there's something missing. That nagging question "What if . . . ?" continues to float in your head. You are afraid that you have forever missed the chance for God to use you. I want you to know that God can still use you, just as He has used others mentioned in this book.

Perhaps you have gone through some terrible tragedy or hardship, and you feel as though God is distant. Maybe you even feel He has let you down. You no longer have the desire to move forward. As you'll see in one of the upcoming chapters, people who have chosen to take God at His word after some severe hardship have seen "all things work together for good" (Romans 8:28).

On the other hand, you may feel as though your fruitful years are over. You don't see how you can do anything productive for His kingdom. You feel that you are too old, too ill, or perhaps too inadequate. In this book you will find that God often chooses to do His greatest work through the most unlikely people. Yes, you have a second chance for service.

Or maybe you feel you don't need a second chance. Perhaps everything is just great in your life—you're happy, you're walking with God, your family life is terrific. God bless you, my friend, but you, more than most, need to know about second chances. Because dark clouds are out there on the horizon. You may not see them yet, but, believe me, they are there. You need to be prepared for the rough times ahead and how they will test you. That's what this book is about. It's a book for everyone, because everyone needs to find forgiveness and second chances at times in their lives.

How do you get second chances? It begins with making the right choices—the kinds of choices you can make right now, right where you are. Are you ready?

acknowLedgments

SPECIAL THANKS to Cathe, my wife, for her always valuable and wise insights. I also wish to thank Greg Denham for the original vision for this book (after hearing a message I gave on a second chance at one of our Harvest Crusades); Mark Ferjulian for his diligence and tenacity in bringing this book to reality; Joseph Farah for his creative help in editing and presentation; Ron Beers and my friends at Tyndale House Publishers for their heart to bring this message to people who need to hear it; my wonderful staff at Harvest for their support and help; and, as always, the congregation of Harvest Christian Fellowship, the church I have had the privilege of pastoring for twenty-nine years. It was to them these messages were first delivered.

†HE GOD OF FORGiVENESS

part 1

A SNAPSHOT
OF GOD

*But while he was still a long way off, his father saw him and was
filled with compassion for him; he ran to his son, threw his arms
around him and kissed him.*
   LUKE 15:20, NIV

Perhaps the classic biblical story of the second chance is the
story of the Prodigal Son.

Some years ago there was a book written titled *All I Ever
Needed to Know I Learned in Kindergarten*. In a similar sense, we
could say, "All I ever needed to know about God I found in the
story of the Prodigal Son."

Now, that's not true in a literal sense, because God has
revealed Himself to us in all of Scripture. Yet so many of the
major themes of the Bible are touched on in this short but powerful picture of who God is and how He feels toward us even when
we have miserably failed. The story of the Prodigal Son gives us
an important glimpse into the nature and character of God.

What is God like? That's a question many people are asking
today. Is He a hostile cosmic killjoy out to make our lives on
this earth miserable, just waiting to throw us into hell? Is He a
benign, all-loving, accepting supreme force with no real opinions
about what we say and do? Or is He a disinterested, disengaged
deity with better things to do than to fool around with you and
me? Actually, none of these ideas comes close to describing
what God is like.

The Bible tells us that God is love. It doesn't say that God is merely loving. It says He is love. He is love personified. He is love incarnate. He is not merely loving in general. His love is directed toward humanity. And on a more personal note, it is directed toward you and me as individuals. God is thinking about us.

"Oh, please!" you might protest. "Surely God has better things to do than to think of me. And even if He did think of me, it would certainly not be with thoughts of love."

The fact is, God thinks about you and loves you deeply. He says, "For I know the thoughts that I think toward you, says the Lord, thoughts of peace and not of evil, to give you a future and a hope. Then you will call upon Me and go and pray to Me, and I will listen to you. And you will seek Me and find Me, when you search for Me with all your heart" (Jeremiah 29:11-13).

Isn't that incredible? It would be more than enough if God had ever even noticed us, much less actually thought about us. Yet, in this great statement God does not merely say that He has thought a single thought about us—even though that would be wonderful! And He doesn't say that He thinks about us occasionally. He says, "For I know the *thoughts* that I think toward you." God is actively and continually thinking about you. In fact, He is thinking about you right now as you read this book.

His thoughts toward you are good, and He has a special plan for your life that is motivated by His undying love for you. The psalmist tells us, "Many, O Lord my God, are Your wonderful works which You have done; and Your thoughts toward us cannot be recounted to You in order; if I would declare and speak of them, they are more than can be numbered" (Psalm 40:5).

Imagine this for a moment: God's thoughts toward you are innumerable. So if sometimes it seems as if your friends and family have forgotten about you, remember you are always on His mind! You might say, "I can believe that God loves me when I am living as I should. But when I fail, when I fall, surely He doesn't love me then." This is simply not true. God's love toward you is not contingent upon what you do. It does not hinge even on how you live. It's there when you flourish spiritually, but it's also there when you're "going down in flames." You might wonder how such a thing could be possible.

Consider now the story that Jesus told to illustrate this great truth. When people hear the story of the Prodigal Son, many immediately focus on the prodigal in the story. We often think of him as the ultimate black sheep of the family—the young boy who miserably failed his father and brought untold shame to family and friends. But there is more than one main character in this story. When Jesus told that now-familiar narrative, He wasn't just emphasizing the plight of the prodigal. He was also highlighting the nature of His heavenly Father. Here Jesus gives us a "snapshot" of God—a picture of God running to embrace a returning wayward child.

That's not the usual picture many have of God. Right now you might be thinking, *But I've done so many horrible things. I've failed God so miserably. There's no way He will take me back.*

That's the way a young woman named Julia felt who attended one of my Bible studies. She later wrote, "Going forward at church was a regular thing with me, but I never really changed. God was always portrayed as a judge who would send us to the lake of fire for the smallest mistake. As I fell further into sin, I figured it was all over for me, but I never wanted it to be over. I'm very ashamed of the things I did and the time I wasted, but that's all behind me. I just want to begin again—take things from square one and move forward." That night at the Bible study, God ran and embraced that prodigal child as she rededicated her life to Christ.

Maybe you don't see God the same way this young woman does. Perhaps you view Him as some distant, impersonal entity or a "judge who would send us to the lake of fire for the smallest mistake." Yet you wish that you could know God in a personal way—to be able to reach out and somehow touch Him.

Who better to illustrate, to personify God's nature, character, and attitude toward us than Jesus Christ? You see, God became "one of us." He became an actual man. And He is touchable, knowable, and closer than you may think.

In John 1:14 we read, "And the Word became flesh and dwelt among us." That's an interesting phrase. It could be translated, "He tabernacled among us," or "He pitched His tent here among us."

It is amazing to stop and think that the creator of the universe—the almighty God, whose origins are from everlasting—came to this earth not only as a man but as a baby. He went from the throne of heaven to a feeding trough. He went from the presence of angels to a cave filled with animals. He who was larger than the universe became an embryo. He who sustains the world with a word chose to be dependent upon the nourishment of a young girl named Mary.

The radical commitment Jesus made in coming to earth is summed up in Philippians 2:6-8: "Although He existed in the form of God, [He] did not regard equality with God a thing to be grasped, but emptied Himself, taking the form of a bond-servant, and being made in the likeness of men. And being found in appearance as a man, He humbled Himself by becoming obedient to the point of death, even death on a cross" (NASB).

Although Jesus was God and He remained God throughout His earthly ministry, He laid aside the privileges of deity. Simply put, He chose to experience the limitations of a human being. If Jesus was hungry, He didn't snap His fingers and have food materialize. He never performed a miracle for His own benefit. He knew complete exhaustion. He knew pain. He knew deep anguish and bitter sorrow.

I heard the story of a little boy who was frightened one

night by a thunderous lightning storm. He called to his father in the other room, "Daddy, I'm scared!"

"Son," the father said reassuringly, "God loves you, and He'll take care of you."

"I know God loves me," the boy replied, "but right now I want somebody who has skin on."

Why do I point this out? So we can know that we have a God who understands what we're going through. When we feel sorry for ourselves, we have no right to pray, "Dear God, You don't know what this is like. You're up there in heaven, and I'm on earth. It's rough down here."

God could easily respond, "But I do know what it's like. I know what you're going through right now. I've been there, and I'm here now for you."

He knows what it is like to face the temptations and struggles of the human life. As Scripture says, "We do not have a High Priest who cannot sympathize with our weaknesses, but was in all points tempted as we are, yet without sin" (Hebrews 4:15). God is not only sympathetic but approachable.

Our Approachable Father
In the story of the Prodigal Son, the father is not only approachable but overwhelmed with joy at the return of his lost son. Look at his reaction to seeing his son in the distance. Luke 15:20 says that while the son was "still a great way off, his father saw him and had compassion." The J. B. Phillips translation says that "his father saw him and his heart went out to him." Does that look like a father bent on making his son pay for the disgrace he has given the family name? Would you say he's a father who has written off his son? Of course not. I see a hurting, caring father—a father who misses his son so much that he actually strains to see him in the distance.

Considering that Jesus used this story to help explain

what God is like, how do you think God feels when we have run away from Him? How does God react when we have broken His commandments? We often want to envision Him as some angry deity ready to throw a lightning bolt at us. Yet, if we follow the picture that Jesus gives us here, God misses us. We have a picture of a father who really wanted his son to come home. Maybe this father would wander into his son's empty room each day and look around. The memories of their precious times together would flood his mind. But now the son was gone, and the father did not know where he was. He missed him every single day. He constantly looked down that road. Hoping. Praying. Waiting. There would be something missing in his life until his son came home. Then one day when the father saw the familiar frame of his son straggling back toward home, his heart leaped with joy.

That's God's attitude toward us when we begin to make a move toward Him. Unlike an earthly father, our Father in heaven knows exactly where we've been and what we've been doing. Our actions and failures come as no surprise to Him. But the good news is that, in spite of our mistakes, shortcomings, and sins, He still loves us. He welcomes us home. He's ready to embrace us and kiss us.

Look again, from the father's perspective, at what the Bible says in Luke 15:20. The boy was a great way off. That's how God see humanity. We are distanced from Him. But, like the father in the story, God saw us when we were far off. And, like that father, He reached out to us: "But now in Christ Jesus you who once were far off have been brought near by the blood of Christ" (Ephesians 2:13).

In essence, that's the message of salvation. Because of the distance between God and us, we just can't get to Him on our own. We can try building our little roads and bridges and ladders, but they all fall short. That is why God reached out to us when He walked among us and went to a cross and died there for our sin. And when we accept Christ and receive Him into our lives, God throws His arms around us and gladly receives us.

You may be a believer already, but one who has backslidden. To put it biblically, you have gone astray.

When people are not doing well spiritually, they usually want to put as much distance as possible between themselves and anything that reminds them of the God they are disobeying. They no longer have time for church, or prayer, or reading the Bible. Then one day they find themselves a great way off, and they can't believe how far they have gone.

When you feel a distance between yourself and God, who do you think has moved? I think you already know the answer. If you sincerely asked the Lord into your life, He promised, "I will never leave you nor forsake you" (Hebrews 13:5). He also loves those who are His children with an "everlasting love" (Jeremiah 31:3).

A Welcome Reunion

Notice the reaction of the prodigal's father when he recognizes his son: He runs to meet him. This is an interesting point. In ancient Hebrew culture it was considered undignified for an older man to run. It was just not done. But this father didn't care about his image. He didn't care about dignity. All he cared about was his son. And that's the way God is. If Jesus had not suggested it, it would seem almost sacrilegious to suggest that God is willing to lose His dignity on our behalf. But that's the picture Jesus paints of God—as an older man, sacrificing his dignity to get to his son as quickly as possible to throw his arms around him. Through the eyes of Jesus, we see a God who loves us so much that He cannot wait to show us His love. Then we read that the father kissed his son. A more accurate translation would be "he smothered his son with kisses." The father kissed him over and over again, even though the son no doubt needed a bath. Don't you think that kid may have stunk a little bit? Keep in mind that he had been hanging around with pigs. Have you ever smelled a pigpen? This kid must have reeked. His clothes had to have been tattered rags. He would have been covered with filth. The father could have easily said, "Son, phew! Go get a bath, then I'll hug you." No. He hugged him and kissed him in his miserable, stinking state.

Some people think that in order to come to God, they have to clean up their lives first—possibly try to be better people, use less profanity, be more considerate. But Jesus doesn't tell us to clean up our lives and then come to Him. In essence, He says, "Come to me, and I will clean up your life," and "The one who comes to Me I will by no means cast out" (John 6:37). One of the songs that is sung at our Harvest Crusades as people are coming forward to commit themselves to Christ is titled "Come Just As You Are." That's how the Prodigal Son came to his father. He came just as he was. We can do the same. Here's the good news: Jesus cleans His fish after He catches them. Come to God as you are. Come with all your sins. Come with your problems. Come in your rags. And God will throw His arms around you.

A God Who Dresses His Children
Please notice something else in this story: The father did not leave the young man in his rags. Instead, he tells his servants, "Bring out the best robe and put it on him, and put a ring on his hand and sandals on his feet" (Luke 15:22). The rags came off, and the new clothes went on.

This verse is significant. I have heard many people say, "God loves me just as I am." That's right. But God doesn't want to leave us that way. We are not to use God's unconditional love as a justification for a lifestyle that is not pleasing to Him.

Although God does love us in spite of all our sins and shortcomings, He wants to change us. Scripture takes this analogy further, saying, "Clothe yourselves with the Lord Jesus Christ, and do not think about how to gratify the desires of the sinful nature" (Romans 13:14, NIV). In other words, we should cast aside or take off those things that have kept us away from God and begin to live a new life as we walk with the Lord.

Taking off the old and putting on the new is a strong analogy that is used repeatedly in the New Testament to describe our new lives in Christ (see Galatians 3:27; Colossians 3:12; 1 Peter 5:5). One might even say that part of the reason people fall so easily into the prodigal situation is their failure to put off the old and put on the new. They try to live in two worlds and quickly find out that it just doesn't work.

Have you heard of the Civil War soldier who couldn't decide which side to support? He put on the blue coat of the North and the gray trousers of the South and went out on the battlefield. He ended up getting shot at from both sides!

So in looking at this story of the Prodigal Son from the father's point of view, we see that God loves us, He accepts us, He wants to forgive us, and He wants to change our lives. So many people fail to grasp these truths because they don't understand what truly happens when they commit their lives to Christ.

An Understanding of Your Standing

When we come to Christ, not only are we forgiven of our sin, but we also are what the Bible calls *justified*. The Bible explains justification in Romans 5:1: "Therefore, since we have been justified through faith, we have peace with God through our Lord Jesus Christ" (NIV).

Salvation has to do with what takes place in believers' hearts, but justification has to do with our standing before God. In salvation God gives us new life. But justification goes beyond that. It is being declared righteous in the sight of God. "Just as if I'd never done it" is one way the word *justified* has been explained. Not only does God forgive us, but it is as if our sin never happened. He removes it, and in its place He puts the perfect righteousness of Christ.

It's as if your checking account were empty, but one day you go to the ATM machine and, just for old time's sake, punch in your code. Suddenly you realize you have a balance of five million dollars!

God has done more than that for you. He has given you His righteousness. You have been justified.

Adopted and Assured

If forgiveness and justification were all that we received by accepting God's gift of salvation, that would be enough. But there's more. God says, "I want you to be my son. I want you to be my daughter." He adopts us into His family.

Salvation has to do with a change in nature. Justification has to do with a change in standing. I have become the Father's child. The Bible says in Romans 8:15-16, "You did not receive a spirit that makes you a slave again to fear, but you received the Spirit of sonship. And by him we cry, 'Abba, Father.' The Spirit himself testifies with our spirit that we are God's children" (NIV).

When the Prodigal Son returned to his father, the father could have said, "Son, it's good to see you again, but you have really embarrassed me. Why don't you go bunk out there with the hired help? I don't want you in the house anymore. Get out of here. By the way, don't refer to me as your father any longer."

He didn't do that. He said, "Son, you are still my son. I missed you, and I welcome you home."

Then he put a ring on his son's finger, which meant that the young prodigal still held his position as his father's son.

Have you been running from God? Are you afraid of what

He will say or do if you come back to Him? God is waiting for you with open arms. He is willing to go to any length to get you back. He is preserving your place in the family. You are still His child. If you return to Him, He will run to you. And He will change you so that you can enjoy all the privileges that are yours as His child.

THE SEEKING
SHEPHERD

Your Father in heaven is not willing that any of these little
ones should be lost.
  MATTHEW 18:14, NIV

Raul Ries was just a boy when he fled Mexico for the United
States. It wasn't so much his impoverished country he was
running from but his circumstances—a home life dominated by
an abusive, alcoholic father who could be extremely cruel to his
family. Raul was also turned off and frustrated by rituals he did
not understand in the church in which he was raised.

Southern California hardly proved to be the Promised
Land. But Ries learned to survive by counting on his ability to
fight. In high school in West Covina he headed up a fierce
Latino street gang. When he crippled a football player from an
opposing team at a party, a judge suggested that a tour of duty
with the Marine Corps would be the only thing that would keep
him out of jail.

Ries turned out to be a good soldier. Killing came easily to
him. He won a Purple Heart and became a kung fu expert. He
even served for a time as a point man—the soldier who walks
ahead of the others and thus faces the greatest danger—for his
crack marine unit. What is amazing is that Ries volunteered for
the job! After a while, killing became even easier as his unit
moved into the thatched villages of the Vietnamese jungle and
just started shooting. He later told me, with tears in his eyes,

15

that the victims had included women and children. He just didn't care anymore.

Unfortunately, the rage, violence, and jungle skills that had proved so useful in Vietnam didn't help Ries adapt to life back in the United States. After returning home, Ries, like the father he had fled from in Mexico, abused his own wife and children. One night he came home to discover that his wife had packed suitcases for herself and the children. If they were leaving, he thought, it would be literally over his dead body.

Ries waited for his family to come home. Sometimes he sat with a loaded rifle in his hands. Sometimes he paced. Sometimes he crouched on the floor like a sniper waiting for his targets to walk in the door. His plan was to kill quickly—his wife, the kids, and then himself. He got angrier as he waited, more certain than ever that there was no other way.

But it was taking so long. What was keeping them? Where were they? In a rage he struck the television with the butt of his rifle. A moment later, almost miraculously, there appeared the beaming face of a man who was describing something Ries knew next to nothing about: Love. The man's name was Chuck Smith, and he was speaking from the pulpit of Calvary Chapel in Costa Mesa, California.

"You see, God is perfect," Chuck was saying. "And in His holiness, He can't have anything to do with us sinners. But He loves us so much that He Himself took the just penalty for all the sins in all of our lives. God wants you to know that, in spite of what you may be, or in spite of what you may have done— you may have messed up your life completely—God still loves you. He is reaching out to you and inviting you to come and to share that love with Him, no matter how deeply you may have gone into sin. Jesus offers forgiveness to us as a free gift. All we have to do is accept it."

On what had been shaping up to be his last night here on

earth, there could not have been a message more suited for
Raul Ries. His heart began pounding with excitement. Something was stirring deep within his soul. He doesn't remember
when he put the gun down. But he does recall kneeling down in
front of the television screen and sincerely praying for forgiveness, all the while sobbing uncontrollably.

But repenting in the privacy of his living room wasn't
enough for Ries. He decided he needed to get down to that
church as fast as he could to make a public confession of his
faith. When the invitation was given to come to Christ, he
nearly ran down the aisle. What he didn't know was that his
wife and kids were at that very service, unaware of the horrible
fate that would have met them had God not miraculously inter-
vened just a few minutes earlier.

Raul Ries experienced the kind of life-changing encounter
with Christ that the apostle Paul had on the road to Damascus.
And, like Paul, Ries dedicated his life to building a life-changing,
Bible-teaching church that has touched countless lives. He is a
completely changed man with a few exceptions: He still has the
same wife, the same kids, the same parents, and some of the
same friends and associates. But those who have witnessed the
dramatic change in his life cannot help but be affected by it.

"So great was Raul's change that those who knew him had
to pinch themselves to make sure that it was not all a dream,"
writes Chuck Smith in his book *Harvest*, coauthored with Tal
Brooke. "And almost all of the people who witnessed Raul's
alarming change are themselves changed because of it. They
have become Christians, and most of them attend Raul's church."

The story does not end there. One night Raul's alcoholic
father walked down the aisle of his church—Calvary Chapel of
West Covina—to dedicate his life to Christ.

"This man who had been so impossible to live with, so
cruel to his family, whom Raul had been an adversary of all his

life, was now changed," writes Smith. "For the child of an alco-holic, such a change represents a miraculous gift. A huge burden was lifted from Raul's shoulders, one he had been carrying all of his life."[1]

A Shepherd on the Lookout for Flailing Sheep

Raul and his father discovered another important aspect of God's character: He seeks out those who are lost. And when-ever we wander from the Savior, He will always come looking for us.

It's no accident that one particular analogy is used repeat-edly throughout the Bible to describe God and his relationship with people. God is often described as a shepherd, and we are often described as sheep, probably for good reason.

If you were to do a little research on sheep, you'd discover that they are completely defenseless and require more care and attention than any other kind of livestock. They also have a mob mentality. They tend to work together in concert. They desperately want to conform. Sound like anyone you know?

A good shepherd looks out for the welfare of his sheep. As David, the shepherd-psalmist, describes in Psalm 23, a good shepherd leads his sheep to the green pastures and beside still waters. In spite of all the shepherd's tender care and good intentions, though, the sheep have another trait that is so much like us. They tend to go astray. As the Scriptures say, "All we like sheep have gone astray; we have turned, every one, to his own way" (Isaiah 53:6).

Perhaps that's why David adds to the list of the Shepherd's duties, "He restores my soul" (Psalm 23:3). You would think that anyone under the care of the Good Shepherd would never go astray or need restoration. But, sadly, that is not the case. Because sheep are also incredibly stupid, they can be spooked by a stray jackrabbit and run in panic, sometimes to their own detriment. Even more amazing, sheep have actually been known to follow one wayward leader over the face of a cliff, one by one, dropping blindly to their death.

It isn't necessarily a compliment that God, on more than one occasion, compares us to these dense, wayward creatures. He could have said, "My chimpanzees hear my voice," comparing us to a relatively intelligent animal. Or perhaps, "My dolphins hear my voice." Everyone who watched Flipper on television remembers that he always saved the day. Or even, "My dogs hear my voice." But no. Jesus said, "My sheep hear my voice." He says that because we are just like them.

Why do we run from God? Why do we disregard His plan for our lives? Isn't it amazing that we break God's commandments, ignore His Word, and then—when we begin to reap what we have sown—actually get angry at God about it? In essence, we blame God for a mess that we ourselves have made, a problem of our own design.

Let's consider why sheep might need to be restored. In Psalm 42:11, David cries out, "Why are you cast down, O my soul? And why are you disquieted within me? Hope in God; for I shall yet praise Him."

The phrase in that verse for "cast down" is an old English shepherd's term for a sheep that has turned itself over on its back and cannot get up again by itself. This would leave the sheep in a vulnerable position, flailing away with its legs. A sheep in such a predicament would make a great target for a predator such as a wolf, coyote, vulture, or buzzard.

It's interesting that the sheep that are the most vulnerable to being cast down are those that are, in politically correct terminology, *well fed*. Or, to put it in plain English, the fat sheep. Phillip Keller, a modern-day shepherd who wrote an insightful book on Psalm 23, explains how this happens: "The heavy, fat sheep will lie down comfortably in some little hollow in the ground and roll on its side slightly to sort of relax. Suddenly the center of gravity in the body will shift so the sheep will turn on its back far enough so the feet no longer touch the ground. The sheep, feeling a sense of panic, begins to paw frantically, and that only makes matters worse. It's a little bit like a turtle being stuck on its shell upside down. He just can't get turned over again," Keller says.[2]

Once this happens, the sheep is in serious trouble, and it will die in a matter of hours. So if the shepherd recognizes that one of his flock is missing, he will go searching for it, knowing that time is of the essence. He looks for signs to direct him to the sheep, such as circling vultures or buzzards that think they are about to have leg of lamb for dinner. The shepherd must get to the sheep as quickly as possible to put it back on its feet—essentially to restore it.

Of course, the sheep had no intention of getting into this dilemma. It started innocently enough. But one thing leads to another, and suddenly it's in desperate need of the shepherd's immediate help. Again, it's the well-fed sheep that are the most vulnerable to being *cast down*. In the same way, often those of us who are the most vulnerable to sin are not the weakest but the strongest.

You say, "What? It seems that the weak believers would be most vulnerable." Well, yes, they can be, but sometimes weak people recognize their vulnerability and, as a result, stay closer to the Shepherd and under His care. But the strong, fat-and-sassy ones, feeling their oats, say, "I don't need to be that close all the time. I will just wander off on my own and kick back over here and take it easy." It's at those moments when we lower our guard that we can be hit by an onslaught of fiery arrows from hell. So we must always keep our guard up. As the Scriptures say, "Let him who thinks he stands take heed lest he fall" (1 Corinthians 10:12).

David himself, the author of Psalm 23, is a case in point. The Bible tells us in 2 Samuel 11 that when the time had come for kings to go forth in battle, David was lounging around on his rooftop patio. He was taking a little R and R when he spied a beautiful woman named Bathsheba bathing herself. You know the rest of that story. As the old song says, "Just one look, that's all it took. . . ."

There's nothing wrong with taking a little vacation. And certainly there's nothing wrong with resting. But timing is everything, and a king should not be on vacation when it's time to lead his troops into battle. In essence David was taking a *spiritual* vacation. He was taking a little time off from walking closely with God and from spiritual pursuits. At this point in his life we don't read about his playing the harp and singing praises to the Lord as he had done as a young shepherd boy out in the hills, where he composed many of his beautiful devotional psalms. Maybe he was resting on his laurels, looking at all the good he had done. Whatever the case, he was like an overfed sheep that lay down to relax, lost its center of gravity, and was suddenly cast down and in desperate need of the shepherd's help.

Do you need restoration right now? Maybe you have strayed into sin or gotten yourself into trouble. You may even think that God is looking for you—hunting you down so He can give you what you deserve. You may think that God operates by that humorous saying "If you love someone, set him free. If he loves you, he will return to you. If he doesn't return to you, hunt him down and kill him!"

Au contraire! God loves you. He misses you. And just as in the story that Jesus told of the shepherd who left the ninety-nine sheep to go after the one that had gone astray, God is seeking you out, wanting to put you back on your feet.

The Christian thinker and writer C. S. Lewis first discovered the depths of the Savior's love and mercy when he finally surrendered his life to God:

> In the Trinity Term of 1929, I gave in and admitted that God was God, and knelt and prayed; perhaps, that night, the most dejected and reluctant convert in all England. I did not then see what is now the most shining and obvious thing; the divine humility which will accept a convert even on such terms. The prodigal son at least walked home on his own feet. But who can duly adore that Love which will open the high gates to a prodigal who is brought in kicking, struggling, resentful, and darting eyes in every direction for a chance of escape? The words *compelle intrare*, "compel them to come in," have been so abused by the wicked men that we shudder at them; but, properly understood, they plumb the depth of divine mercy. The hardness of God is kinder than the softness of men, and His compulsion is our liberation.[3]

God is just as patient toward His wayward child as He is toward the reluctant convert. Consider again the image of restoring a flailing sheep. The shepherd goes to the cast-down sheep, wraps his arms around it, tilts it back onto its feet, and gently begins to massage its legs, getting the blood circulating again. All the while, the shepherd speaks to the sheep in soothing tones, correcting it but loving it.

God wants to put you back on your feet. He loves you. He's seeking you. If you need restoration, turn to the Good Shepherd today. He wants to restore you and lovingly bring you back into the fold.

†HE MAKING
OF A
PRODiGAL

part 2

THE PULL OF
THE WORLD

*The one who received the seed that fell among the thorns is
the man who hears the word, but the worries of this life and
the deceitfulness of wealth choke it, making it unfruitful.*
MATTHEW 13:22, NIV

What makes a prodigal? More specifically, what makes our spir
itual life less than what it should really be? Why would we want
to look for happiness anywhere other than in our relationship
with Christ? Let's go back to the story of the prodigal for some
answers. He shows us the perils of what can happen when we
look for happiness outside the protective haven of our heavenly
Father.

As the story begins, we find a young man deciding to leave
home. We really don't know much about this boy, but many of
us envision a rebellious teenager coming into his own. In effect,
he says, "Look, I'm tired of the constraints and the restrictions
of living here at home with you, Dad. I want to go out there and
live life the way I choose to live it. I'm tired of being here under
your roof. I want my portion of the estate that is coming to me."

We don't know what led to this boy wanting to leave
home. In fact, his home seemed like a secure and loving place.
It clearly was an affluent home, but not at the expense of love
and affection displayed by the father. This was not like so many
homes in America today where fathers have abandoned their
kids. Nor was the father too busy to take time for his son. The

young boy in this story knew no such deprivation. Instead, he appears to be simply a self-centered kid who thought he knew more than his father.

Keep in mind that it was very difficult in those days to divide an estate while the father was still living. But this boy evidently didn't care about inconveniencing his father. He didn't care about what heartache or what difficulty it would bring. All he cared about was himself and his demands.

The father could have easily denied him. He could have said, "You're not going anywhere, Son. And if you try to go, I will deal harshly with you." Instead, this loving father, who understood the risks, allowed his son to exercise his own free will, and the son was more than happy to do just that. He set out to find his own way. It appears that he had lost confidence in his father. To the boy's warped way of thinking, his father stood between him and what he thought he really wanted—something unidentifiable in the outside world beyond his father's estate. Maybe he was tired of school or work or his responsibilities. So off he went because the bright lights of the big city were beckoning.

When he went out the front door, he didn't even offer a word of thanks. He didn't hug his father and say, "Dad, thanks for all of those years when you took care of me and provided for me. I want you to know I still love you; I'm just a bit confused right now."

No, he just left. He was out of there as fast as his prodigal little legs could carry him. There was probably a sense of liberation about it all. Freedom. He was on his own and going to live free and easy. No more curfews or fatherly lectures. No more rules or regulations. No more having his style cramped. Just complete freedom to do what he wanted to do, with whom he wanted to do it, whenever he felt like it. He would find out in good time that vice has a price.

This is a picture of our relationship—or lack thereof—with God. We say, "I don't want God's constraints in my life. I don't want to live by what the Bible teaches. I want to find my own way." Like the father of the Prodigal Son, God has given us free will. He won't force us to stay close to Him. He doesn't say, "If you wander from Me, I'm going to beat you up or strike you blind." He essentially says, "I love you, and it hurts Me deeply when you stray from Me, but I want you to follow Me out of choice, not coercion." It breaks His heart when we leave Him. It hurts Him deeply when we sin against Him and violate His commandments. But God will allow us to make our own choices and reap the consequences.

Like the Prodigal Son, many of us are ungrateful for all that God offers us. It amazes me how flippant we can be in considering God's gracious offer of forgiveness. We act as if we have all the resources and time in the world. We act as if we are almost doing God a favor by even considering Christianity.

Perhaps we envision ourselves sitting in a fine restaurant at a well-placed table, complete with a crisp linen tablecloth and polished silverware. Soft music is gently playing in the background. We are slowly perusing the menu, but instead of food, this restaurant offers the various religious beliefs of the world. We decide to order à la carte.

"Okay, Waiter. Hmmm, let's see. I would like a small order of Christianity. Hold the guilt, please. I'm on a guilt-free diet. I'll have a side order of Hinduism. Another side order of Buddhism. And could you season that with some New Age spices, please?" We often just make up the rules as we go, picking and choosing what appeals to us as we casually peruse the celestial menu of religion.

But here's the real picture. You are not at some fine table choosing from a menu where "all roads lead to God." You are in the middle of a burning hot desert, and you are severely dehydrated. In fact, you're on the verge of death. You have no resources to purchase food or water. You have no options. You are dying.

Suddenly God appears before you. In the coolness of the shade, He sets a beautiful table with the finest, freshest gourmet offerings in the universe, and He bids you to come and dine. The price for the sumptuous feast has already been paid. All you have to do is take a seat and feast away.

Notice that there are no other options. It's simple—eat and live, or don't eat and die. That's reality. God offered only one way for us to be forgiven of our sins. He came to earth, walked among us, went to a cross, and died there in our place. We are not doing God a favor by considering His offer of salvation. He is doing us a favor by offering it in the first place! We should all be running to Him to receive His offer of forgiveness—before it's too late.

The Attractiveness of the Forbidden

The Prodigal Son didn't want to be around his family or his father. They probably irritated him. I can just hear him saying, "Hey man, you are cramping my style. I don't like all the rules around this place. It makes me uncomfortable."

A lot of people feel that way about Christians. "I don't like to go to church," they say. "Christians are so narrow-minded. They are so restrictive. Too many rules. They are too serious. I don't want to live that way." In reality, they want to get away from anyone or anything that reminds them of God. When we invite these people to church, they will offer a plethora of excuses because they don't really want to come at all. Have you ever heard the definition of an excuse? An excuse is the skin of a reason stuffed with a lie. We offer excuses when we don't want to participate. Excuses betray a complete lack of desire or interest.

The Prodigal Son wanted to get away from his father. He didn't want to change his lifestyle to conform with his father's will. He wasted what he had on prodigal—wasteful—living. He probably left home with a spring in his step and money in his pocket. When he hit town, I bet he was one popular guy. But the money quickly ran out, along with his fair-weather friends.

He also lived immorally, consorting with prostitutes. He indulged himself with whatever money could buy. I can just hear him saying, "You only go around once." But when all the money was gone, he was reduced to nothing. He hit bottom fast.

That's what happens when we begin looking to the things of this world for our happiness. Many people today feel that if they had more money they would be happy. ABC News produced a program that dealt with the subject of happiness, titled "The Mystery of Happiness: Who Has It . . . How to Get It." The program began by asking, "What is happiness?"

One man said, "A hundred million dollars."

A woman stated, "More ready cash."

Another man said, "A castle."

Another answered, "A private island."

And, of course, a man said, "A bunch of women."

It sounds to me as if they were taking cues from the Prodigal Son!

The host of the program, John Stossel, stated: "Americans have time to think about it, and we seem to have become increasingly convinced that maybe money will buy happiness. Twenty-five years ago, when college students were asked what's important, most said 'family,' or 'developing a meaningful life and philosophy.' But today most students say it is being well-off financially."

The program went on to show, however, that even winning the lottery is no guarantee for happiness. As Stossel reported, "Studies of lottery winners found that within a year most say they are no happier than they were before they won."

One man, Curtis Sharpe, who had collected $5 million in

the New York lottery, said, "For a while it seemed like I was in a dream world, you know?"

"Did you come down to earth?" he was asked.

"Oh yes," he replied. "I came down to earth. I got divorced from my first wife and married my second wife, and I spent a lot of money on the wedding—a hundred thousand dollars. Only that didn't last five years. You know what I'm saying?"

We might conclude that he didn't win quite enough. But Sherry Gagliardi and her husband won $26 million, and their story didn't turn out much better.

"I was numb for three years," she said.

"But you must have been happy," the interviewer said.

"Yes and no," she replied. "I got a divorce two years after we won."

"Can money buy you happiness?" she was asked.

"Of course not," she said. "It could buy you a therapist— you know, a marriage counselor. People have a misconception about having money. You go out and say, 'That's what I want; I'll buy it.' Then a couple of weeks later the emptiness comes back. Then what?"

Professor David Meyers, who spent six years examining hundreds of studies on happiness, says, "Once you get past poverty, money doesn't help, no matter how much stuff you buy—the stockpiles of CDs, the closets full of clothes, the big-screen stereo-TV systems. But clearly that doesn't do it. People, having achieved that level of wealth, have now adapted to it, and it takes new increments, a faster computer, a bigger TV screen, or whatever, to rejuice the joy that the initial purchase gained for them."

A Means to an Empty End

Things haven't changed much in two thousand years, have they? The Prodigal Son found out the hard way that money and

30

sex didn't fulfill his life. Then, to make matters worse, a famine swept the land (Luke 15:14). Isn't that an apt description of what happens when we toy with sin? There will always arise a famine. By that I mean that sin will be fun for a time, and then you will see it for what it really is. Sin is a lot like candy-coated poison. It tastes good at first. When you first dabble with something that may be forbidden, there is an excitement, a fascination with the unknown and forbidden. "Oooh, I'm not supposed to do this, and I'm doing it. I haven't gotten in any trouble yet, and it's more fun than I thought it would be." It's almost liberating in a way. The world is your oyster. But then suddenly the oyster closes in on you.

This is why so many people who experiment with drugs get into harder and more dangerous drugs over time. First they play around. Maybe they smoke a little marijuana. That's exciting to them at first. Then they begin to see how empty and unfulfilling it actually is. So maybe they try cocaine. Or maybe they try LSD. Even heroin. Then one day they wake up as addicts who have lost their way in life. They didn't plan it that way. But that's the inevitable pattern of sin. It always takes you down—down to rock bottom.

The same scenario applies to sexual immorality. When people start fooling around, at first it may be exciting. After a while, though, they need more bizarre and perverse sexual activities and lifestyles to satisfy them. They go deeper and deeper into the vortex of sin because it never satisfies their deepest needs.

I read an almost unbelievable story about a young man named Jordan Lazelle, eighteen, of England. Jordan had been hospitalized after being stung on the tongue by his pet scorpion when he tried to give it its usual good-night kiss.

Lazelle said that when he kissed Twiggy (that was the scorpion's name), it grabbed his lip. Then, when he opened his mouth in shock, "It jumped in and stung me on the tongue. It had never done that before."

This seems incredibly stupid to me, but similarly, how intelligent is it to play with sin? We may rationalize it by saying, "Well, it's only a little sin. It's not really that bad—and, besides, everybody is doing it." Don't you remember your mother's counsel for life? Along with "Always wear clean underwear in case you're in an accident" was the well-worn gem in response to the "everybody's doing it" excuse: "If everybody jumped off a building, would you jump, too?" By the way we sometimes act, the answer would probably be yes. We give some rationalized sin its little good-night kiss and then one night, without warning, it stings us hard! So the famine came for the Prodigal Son.

When you get down to it, there will always be a famine. Sooner *and* later you will come to see this world for what it is— an empty pursuit. Sadly, for many it comes too late. They waste their entire lives. That's what sin does. It chews us up and spits us out. It's so appealing at first. We're young and we say, "It won't happen to us." But look at those who have come out on the other end. Look at what it has done to them. Is that what we want for our future?

The reality may dawn on us rather gradually. We may be at a party surrounded by friends. As we look around we realize how empty it all is. We know that many of these people talk about us behind our backs. (And we talk behind theirs as well.) We see what a dead-end street it all is. Ultimately, everybody has to experience that realization for themselves.

The Bible says, in Ecclesiastes 9:3, "The hearts of men, moreover, are full of evil and there is madness in their hearts while they live, and afterward they join the dead" (NIV). What an appropriate statement. There is madness in the hearts of people living for sin.

Over a period of time the Prodigal Son came to his senses.

He saw it for himself. He realized that the life he was living was not what life was all about. It was ultimately the famine that drove him back into the comfort and protection of his father's home. Originally, he thought he had it tough in his father's house, but then he came to realize that life outside of his father's house was insane.

Many people are raised in Christian homes, hear the truth of the Bible and the commandments of God, and conclude, "That's so restrictive. I don't want to live that way." Then some of them go out, live the way they want, and ultimatcly come back to say, "You know what? God and those commandments make sense. I see that God knows what He's talking about when He says that a man should be faithful to his wife, and a wifc should be faithful to her husband. I see that God knows what Hc's talking about when He tells us we should be honest and responsible." God doesn't give us these standards to make us miserable. He gives them to liberate us—to free us, to help us live life to its fullest. Those are not bars you see holding us in. They are protective barriers that God puts around our lives to keep evil out, to keep us close to Him, to keep us safe.

Finding Happiness God's Way

Philosopher Eric Hoffer writes, "The search for happiness is one of the chief sources of unhappiness." I think there is a lot of truth in that statement. We can actually become very unhappy people as we try to become happy.

The Bible offers a completely different view of happiness than this world gives. According to the Scriptures, happiness is never something that should be sought directly. It's always something that results from seeking something else. It's a by-product. If we seek holiness, we will find happiness. Or, as Jesus said in the Beatitudes, "Blessed are those who hunger and thirst for righteousness, for they will be filled" (Matthew 5:6, NIV). Since the words *blessed* and *happy* are used interchangeably in Scripture, this verse could be translated, "Those who hunger and thirst after righteousness will be happy people."

In other words, true happiness comes from getting our lives right with God. As our will is aligned with His, our lives will find their proper balance. Happiness is not based on circumstances; it's a deep, supernatural contentedness based on the fact that our lives are right with God.

This definition flies in the face of the popular notion that in order to be happy we have to have a perfect physique. To be happy we need to be incredibly wealthy. To be happy we need to be successful. As the Prodigal Son discovered, happiness based on circumstances is elusive. Like it says in Matthew 13:22, the enticements of this world can choke our spiritual growth if left unchecked.

How do we avoid these traps? Psalm 1:1-3 explains:

> Blessed is the man [or, "Oh, the happiness of the man"] who walks not in the counsel of the ungodly, nor stands in the path of sinners, nor sits in the seat of the scornful; but his delight is in the law of the Lord, and in His law he meditates day and night. He shall be like a tree planted by the rivers of water, that brings forth its fruit in its season, whose leaf also shall not wither; and whatever he does shall prosper.

If we want to be happy in the truest way, having a deep contentment and sense of fulfillment and purpose in life—if we want the contentedness that comes from a right relationship with God—we must first avoid things that can be perilous to us spiritually. We need to guard ourselves against anything that hinders our spiritual growth.

Guidelines to Remember

Scripture gives us some guidelines to think about when we have questions about certain activities.

1. *Does it build us up spiritually?* 1 Corinthians 10:23 says, " 'Everything is permissible'—but not everything is beneficial. 'Everything is permissible'—but not everything is constructive" (NIV). *The Twentieth Century New Testament* goes even further, saying, "Everything is allowable! Yes, but everything does not build up character."

When we come face-to-face with a questionable activity, we often ask the wrong questions. Instead of asking, "Is it allowable?" we should be asking, "Is it spiritually constructive?" Instead of trying to find out how much we can "get away with," we need to see if it will promote growth in our Christian character.

The wise man of Psalm 1 does not walk in the counsel of the ungodly, stand in the way of sinners, or sit in the seat of the scornful. He avoids certain things that can hurt him in his spiritual life. Certain relationships, activities, and possessions can spiritually tear us down. Steer clear of anything that would keep you from Christian fellowship, dull your desire for prayer, take away your appetite for Bible study, or make this world more attractive.

2. *Does it bring us under its power?* This guideline is found in 1 Corinthians 6:12, where Paul says, "All things are lawful for me, but all things are not helpful. All things are lawful for me, but I will not be brought under the power of any."

To follow this principle is not to be overly restricted but to live in true freedom. We don't want to be under the power of anything or anyone but Jesus Christ. Because we treasure our relationship with God and the ensuing freedom from sin, we need to guard it jealously. Don't let anything get in its way.

3. *Do I have an uneasy conscience about it?* In those areas where we are uncertain—those so-called "gray areas" of the

Christian life—we might look at them in light of Romans 14:23, which says, "Whatever is not from faith is sin." Another translation of the same verse says, "If you do anything you believe is not right, you are sinning" (NLT).

Have you ever started doing something and felt one of those checks in your heart? You know what I'm talking about—it just doesn't seem right. Immediately you begin to rationalize and say to God, "But God, everybody is doing it. So-and-so does it." Suddenly you realize you sound like a whining teenager.

If we do something but don't have the conviction that God's approval is on it, what is not necessarily a sin for others can be a sin for us. I know that seems strange. Certain things are sinful for everyone, without question. And then there are certain areas that pose a greater problem for some than for others. God wants us to follow the conviction of His Spirit in our personal decisions.

The Prodigal's undoing began with his unhealthy attraction to the world—a curiosity about what he would find outside the confines of his father's house. We don't have to settle for the world's cheap imitations of happiness if we understand what we truly have in our Father's house.

The world offers so-called friends. Most of them stab us in the back, tear us down, or betray us. God offers us a new family—the church—brothers and sisters in God's family who really do care about us. Even though the church has problems, it's far better than anything the shallow world has to offer. "Behold, how good and how pleasant it is for brethren to dwell together in unity!" (Psalm 133:1).

The world offers lust—people hop from bed to bed looking for love. God offers true love—a committed relationship with someone you love and with someone who loves you. "Many waters cannot quench love, nor can the floods drown it" (Song of Solomon 8:7).

The world offers a fleeting happiness largely dependent upon circumstances. God offers joy and contentment, regardless of circumstances. "Happy are the people whose God is the Lord!" (Psalm 144:15).

The world offers drugs and alcohol to dull our pain and supposedly bring fulfillment. In reality, they expand our pain and rob us of real peace. God says, "Do not be drunk with wine, . . . but be filled with the Spirit" (Ephesians 5:18).

The world offers pleasures that are passing and temporal and leave people feeling guilty and destroyed. God offers pleasure and joy that lasts for eternity, giving us eternal hope. "In Your presence is fullness of joy; at Your right hand are pleasures forevermore" (Psalm 16:11).

The Father's house—that's the place to be and stay. There's no place like home.

AN INCOMPLETE
SURRENDER

*No servant can serve two masters. Either he will hate the
one and love the other, or he will be devoted to the one and
despise the other.*
    LUKE 16:13, NIV

Oscar Laurie was a successful man. He had lived a long, full life
and was in the process of entering retirement. Then something
he had not planned upset his life dramatically. While driving his
car one day, he had a heart attack and crashed into a tree. He
could have easily been killed.

After extensive tests he was told that he now had a serious
heart condition and things would never be the same again, not
to mention the ever-present threat of death. That's when my
family came back into his life.

You see, Oscar Laurie adopted me when I was about eight
years old. He not only became my legal father, he also took
an active hands-on role as my functioning father. Oscar, my
mother, and I lived in Summit, New Jersey, where he practiced
law. The most devastating day in my life was when he and my
mom divorced and I, for all practical purposes, lost contact with
him. I thought about him often, but I didn't know where he was
or how he was doing.

After I married my wife, Cathe, I was asked to speak in
New York City, which I gladly agreed to do because I wanted to
see if I could locate my father. A young woman in our church,

who worked as a legal assistant, located him for me through the New York Bar Association. I obtained his office phone number in New Jersey.

I couldn't quite muster up the courage to call him before we left. I wasn't totally sure I would go through with contacting him when we arrived in New York, but I took the number with me just in case. What if he didn't want to talk to me? He probably had his own family, and I didn't want to disrupt that. However, I finally broke down and called his office. His secretary answered.

"Is Oscar Laurie there, please?" I asked.

"Who may I ask is calling?" she responded.

"Greg Laurie."

"How do you spell your last name?"

"The same way he spells his name—L-A-U-R-I-E. This is his son calling!"

My boldness surprised me. She took my number, and he called me back. I wanted to make it easy on him, so I suggested we just grab some lunch together while I was in town. He would have none of that. He insisted that Cathe and I come to his house in New Jersey and stay the weekend. He wanted me to meet his wife, Barbara, and two sons, Jimmy and Bobby. I reluctantly agreed.

As we boarded the train, I had mixed emotions. What would I say to him? Should I still call him Dad?

When our train pulled into the station, there he stood. He looked basically the same as always but with a few new wrinkles. I again surprised myself by hugging him and calling him Dad. He called me Son. It was as if we had never been apart.

It was a wonderful East Coast day with a chill in the air as we made our way to his home. Barbara received us warmly and made us feel welcome with a fantastic Italian dinner that night. As we sat around the table, Barbara, a devout Catholic, asked me what had happened in my life that resulted in my becoming a minister. I shared with her and my father the story of my conversion and how I had given my life to Jesus Christ at the age of seventeen as a confused, empty teenager looking for meaning and purpose in my life.

I remember that as I talked, Barbara was animated and very attentive to what I was saying, whereas my father sat at the other end of the table with his hands pressed together—carefully, analytically listening, much as a judge would hear a case. He was, after all, a lawyer. He was also a moral man. He believed in honesty and was widely known as a man of integrity—not the easiest type of person to reach with the gospel.

Before we went to bed that night, my father asked if I would walk with him in the morning. Ever since his heart attack he had to exercise regularly and maintain a strict diet. I gladly agreed. That night Cathe and I prayed for Oscar and Barbara. I thought she was really open to what I had said, but I wasn't too sure about him.

The next morning came fast, and when Dad knocked on my door, I was in a dead sleep.

"Let's take that walk, Son."

I stumbled out of bed, dressed, and walked into the crisp morning air still half-asleep. We walked for a few minutes before my father made a statement that I could hardly believe. "Greg," he said, "I've been thinking all night about what you said at the dinner table about how Jesus Christ came into your life. I was wondering if you could tell me how to become a Christian."

That woke me up fast! As we continued our walk through the beautiful tree-lined streets of his neighborhood, I proceeded to tell him what it meant to follow Jesus Christ.

"It really comes down to praying and asking Him in," I said in conclusion.

We were standing in a large park. Much to my surprise, Dad dropped to his knees and said, "I'm ready to pray right now!"

I quickly dropped to my knees and led him in prayer. When we finished, with tears coursing down his cheeks, he said, "Jesus just came into my life, Greg!" His whole countenance changed before my eyes. "Can we pray that God will heal my heart condition as well?"

"Well, of course, Dad," I said.

We prayed, and he said, "I believe Jesus has healed my heart!"

"Well, we don't know for sure," I cautioned.

He would hear none of it. "Let's go and tell my doctor. His office is near here!"

I reluctantly agreed, and off we went. He stormed into his doctor's office, boldly proclaiming, "Doctor, this is my son from California. He's a minister, and we just prayed. Jesus Christ came into my life, and I believe he healed my heart, too!"

To be honest, I was a little bit embarrassed. *What if God had not healed him?* I thought.

The doctor ran some tests on him, and guess what? God had not only come into his life but had touched his heart as well.

Dad was sixty-five when he asked Christ into his life. The Lord gave him fifteen more wonderful years to live, during which time Barbara and Jimmy and Bobby all came to believe as well. He was actively involved in his church and led others to Christ. He even became part of the Gideons and helped distribute Bibles to people.

It's never too late. God gave my father a second chance just as He will to anyone else. The Bible is full of stories about people who received second chances when they totally surrendered to Him.

Without Compromise
As Nebuchadnezzar looked over his vast domain, his chest swelled with pride. He let out a sigh of contentment. To say this

man had a life of affluence is the understatement of the year. He had everything a person could possibly want to be happy—unparalleled wealth, power, and fame. He was the king of the most powerful nation on earth at that time—the kingdom of Babylon. Yet he had one serious flaw. He failed to glorify the God who had given him such prestige and power.

Nebuchadnezzar had seen God at work and had been exposed to the truth of God's Word. He was the one who overtook Israel and put the Jewish people into captivity. Among those taken were Shadrach, Meshach, Abed-Nego, and Daniel. They were part of what Nebuchadnezzar deemed the cream of the crop among the young male captives, and they were brought into his court to be schooled in the ways of Babylon.

When these four committed Hebrew teenagers were brought into his court, the king told them to eat of his table, which was a great honor. But when Daniel, Shadrach, Meshach, and Abed-Nego found out what he was offering them, they realized it would be a compromise for them to eat those things (Daniel 1:3-21). It might have been that these foods had been offered to idols, or that they were unclean under the Mosaic law. Whatever the case, these four teenagers took a stand and said, "We will not eat of the king's table." That was a dangerous thing to do with a man like Nebuchadnezzar, a man known to be intolerant. Yet God supernaturally sustained them as they chose a diet of vegetables and water over the fineries of the king's table. In that instance, Nebuchadnezzar witnessed the preserving power of God to those who refuse to compromise.

Later in his reign, the king had a dream that none of his astrologers or magicians could interpret. When he brought young Daniel in to help, Daniel was able to tell him the dream itself, as well as what it meant. Seeing the hand of God on Daniel's life, Nebuchadnezzar acknowledged that Daniel's God was the God of gods: "Truly your God is the God of gods, the

Lord of kings, and a revealer of secrets, since you could reveal this secret" (2:47).

Respect with No Repentance

Although the king acknowledged the power and wisdom of Daniel's God, it apparently had little effect upon the focus of his worship. In Daniel 3 we read about the gold statue that Nebuchadnezzar had erected on the plain of Dura. He then decreed that every person under his domain should fall down and worship the gold image. Obviously, the king's loyalty to God was no more than lip service.

When the music started and everybody bowed down in unison, Shadrach, Meshach, and Abed-Nego stood defiantly amid the sea of prostrate bodies, unwilling to pay homage. As the familiar Bible story relates, the king brought them in and ordered them to bow. Again they refused. The king, who had shown great respect for God when Daniel interpreted his dream, now challenged this same God by boastfully adding, "Who is the god who will deliver you from my hands?" (3:15).

He was about to find out. The king ordered that the furnace be heated seven times hotter than normal. And he commanded some of his mightiest men to throw the three defiant boys into the scorching flames. The heat from the inferno was so intense that his soldiers were overwhelmed and burned to death on the spot.

Surely the three young men would die in seconds, the king thought. But to his astonishment, instead of three bodies in a burning heap at the bottom of the furnace, Nebuchadnezzar saw four people walking around. "The form of the fourth," he said, "is like the Son of God" (3:25).

The king of Babylon gained a newfound respect for the God of these Hebrew men. This time, he went one step further in his public confession of the power of God, saying:

> Blessed be the God of Shadrach, Meshach, and Abed-Nego, who sent His Angel and delivered His servants who trusted in Him, and they have frustrated the king's word, and yielded their bodies, that they should not serve nor worship any god except their own God! Therefore I make a decree that any people, nation, or language which speaks anything amiss against the God of Shadrach, Meshach, and Abed-Nego shall be cut in pieces, and their houses shall be made an ash heap; because there is no other God who can deliver like this. (Daniel 3:28-29)

How like many people today. Oh, they know all the right things to say. They may have even gone forward during an invitation to receive Christ at a church meeting. But in their heart of hearts Jesus is not Lord. They have, for all practical purposes, made an incomplete surrender of their lives to God. And they are usually the most miserable people. Consider this letter I received from a man named John who listens to my radio program:

> Yes, I believe in Jesus. Yes, I've been backsliding most of my Christian life, but I know in my heart I still need to turn two things over to Him and die to my own [selfish] desires. So since 1985 when I accepted Christ, with the exception of six months or so, I have been on the down side of things— backsliding. I ask that you may pray that I may use the strength I know God has given me to stay committed. I don't know if I've ever even known what a true relationship with Christ is.

More Than Lip Service
To be a true follower and believer in God takes more than simply believing that He is Almighty God. It takes *knowing* Him

as your personal Lord and Savior and following His life and words. The Bible says, "Even the demons believe—and tremble!" (James 2:19). Nebuchadnezzar acknowledged the existence of God. But when he was in trouble, he also called out to sorcerers, astrologers, and magicians. You might say that the king wanted to have all the bases covered.

Elvis Presley reportedly wore a cross, a star of David, and other religious medals around his neck. Somebody once asked him, "Elvis, why do you wear all of those? What is your religious belief?"

He replied, "Well, I don't want to miss getting into heaven on a technicality."

And that was Nebuchadnezzar: "I believe in them all. Daniel's God—He is wonderful. The astrologers are fine, too. So are all these beliefs." His thoughts mirror a popular mind-set in our society today: If you have someone representing everything, you're bound to get the truth in there somewhere.

Statistics of Americans who claim to believe in God have never been higher. According to a CNN/Gallup poll, 90 percent of Americans believe in heaven. That's up 6 percent from 1981. Some 79 percent believe in miracles, and 72 percent believe in angels. We say, "That sounds as if we are having a revival." But look closer. A full 27 percent of Americans believe in reincarnation. That's up from 21 percent in 1990. Another 28 percent of Americans believe in contact with the dead. And 10 percent believe Elvis is still alive! Some people believe everything. That's the problem.

A magazine article examining the surge of spirituality in America pointed out that baby boomers are coming back to church in record numbers. But they are also turning to other belief systems as well. While some boomers return to their childhood religions, others seek new meaning outside their own cultures, concocting their own spiritual stew. That's what we have today—just a religious conglomeration of all types of ideas and concepts.

Nebuchadnezzar knew what was right. He simply had not acted upon it. Then one night something as simple as a dream penetrated this king's heart and mind. Daniel had been faithfully sowing his seeds of truth in the king's life over the years. Year after year went by as Nebuchadnezzar persisted in his unbelief. But sometimes the messages we share with others are like little time bombs. They may go off long after they have been preached. One of Daniel's time bombs was about to detonate. It hadn't all been in vain.

Daniel 4 recounts the details of the king's dream as well as the ensuing events that led to his ultimate conversion and surrender to God. In short, it is Nebuchadnezzar's testimony. He begins with the profound statement "I thought it good to declare the signs and wonders that the Most High God has worked for me. How great are His signs, and how mighty His wonders! His kingdom is an everlasting kingdom, and His dominion is from generation to generation" (Daniel 4:2-3).

The Breaking of a King, the Humbling of a Heart
How did pompous, arrogant Nebuchadnezzar come to make this humble acknowledgment regarding the God of Israel? After all, Daniel 4:4 says, "I, Nebuchadnezzar, was at rest in my house, and flourishing in my palace"—and talk about a palace! The king had it made.

Archaeologists have uncovered many of the ruins of Babylon, and it was an incredible place. After Nebuchadnezzar conquered most of the civilized world, he turned his energies back to Babylon. And with all the wealth he had accumulated and the slave labor he had acquired from his conquests, he had unparalleled opportunity to do whatever he desired.

Babylon was home to some of the architectural wonders of

the world. For instance, the walls of Babylon were 350 feet high and 87 feet wide—wide enough for six chariots to race around them side by side. There were one hundred gates throughout the city, each made of burnished bronze. One palace alone covered eleven acres. One banquet hall seated ten thousand people. The outer walls of the city and the walls encircling the buildings inside the city were covered with hand-painted enameled tiles depicting various scenes from Babylonian history. It was truly something to behold.

Although Nebuchadnezzar was safe behind the towering walls of his massive palace and protected by guards who would come at his beck and call, God penetrated it all and got to his heart. The king was troubled by a dream. Some of the hardest people to reach are those who are at rest in their houses—those who, because of all they have, may not see their real spiritual condition. That is why it is a mistake to share the gospel only with unhappy, empty, and lonely individuals. Some people's lives may be going relatively well, like this king's.

So Nebuchadnezzar had this dream—a new dream—and this one was interesting. He dreamed of a massive tree that grew very tall, reaching into the heavens. Birds came and nested in it, and animals found shade under it. Then suddenly without warning the tree shriveled, and the form became a man who was like a beast in the field. Nebuchadnezzar thought, *What is this all about?*

He called in the experts of the occult. In marched the soothsayers, magicians, and astrologers, but they could not explain the dream. Finally, as a last resort, the king brought in Daniel.

As the king unveiled his dream and the Lord gave him the interpretation, Daniel thought, *This is not good.* He realized that the tree represented Nebuchadnezzar and that the king was going to be brought down. He would become like an animal, losing his sensibilities and his mental faculties. Daniel realized that this dream spoke of a certain judgment that was coming to the king. How tempting it would have been to say, "I don't know the interpretation. I just can't give you an answer," because the news was so bad. But Daniel told the king the truth, even though it wasn't easy.

Likewise, Christians have a message to give to those who are not following Christ, and it's not always an easy one. God loves humanity. He is ready to forgive all people who turn from their sins and come to Him by faith through Jesus Christ. But if we are going to be faithful to declare the whole counsel of God, we must tell people that if they reject His loving offer, they seal their own fate and secure their judgment.

In Daniel 4:27 Daniel says something very significant: "Therefore, O king, let my advice be acceptable to you; break off your sins by being righteous, and your iniquities by showing mercy to the poor. Perhaps there may be a lengthening of your prosperity." In essence Daniel was saying, "King, I have some good news. There is a window of opportunity here for you. God's judgment is coming upon you, but if you will repent of your sins, God will spare you. There is a way out, Nebuchadnezzar. If you will repent of your sin, you don't have to end up in the field eating grass like an animal."

Understand this: God doesn't want to judge us. If He wanted to, He would have done it already. Scripture tells us that He takes no delight in the death of the wicked. God is "not willing that any should perish but that all should come to repentance" (2 Peter 3:9). The last thing He wants to do is drop His hammer of judgment on our lives. He doesn't want to see a single person go to the very real place called hell. He doesn't want to see our lives wasted and thrown away. We were made in His image. He cares about us. That is why He sent His own Son to die on the cross in our place.

In the same way, God told the people during Noah's time that judgment was coming. He said, "I will destroy the world." But 120 years passed before it happened. It shows that God is not in a rush for judgment. Still, there comes a moment when the hammer drops and our number is up. There comes a time when we reap what we sow.

Nebuchadnezzar had twelve months to get it together. But he thought, *I'll get away with it. After all, I'm Nebuchadnezzar. I'm the king of Babylon. Who is more powerful than I am?*

The Bible says, "When a crime is not punished, people feel it is safe to do wrong" (Ecclesiastes 8:11, NLT). We may get away with something and think, *I'll never get caught.* But know this: It may be ten years from now; it may be ten hours from now; it may be ten minutes from now. But one thing is certain: Eventually we will reap what we sow. God will keep His word. We can take that to the bank.

Nebuchadnezzar was a wicked man, and he did deserve judgment. He was ready to butcher an entire class of men just because they could not tell him a dream that he had forgotten. He was ready to put to death any who would not worship the golden image that he had erected. He made King Zedekiah, the king of Jerusalem who had rebelled against Babylonian rule, witness the execution of his own two sons. And then, after Zedekiah's sons were killed before their father's very eyes, Nebuchadnezzar had Zedekiah's eyes gouged out so that the last thing this poor king remembered seeing was the slaughter of his sons.

Nebuchadnezzar was a hard man. A vicious man. A wicked man. He deserved judgment. Yet God was offering him a way out of judgment if only he would repent. But he refused.

Daniel 4:29-31 explains the moment when God's judgment came: "At the end of the twelve months he was walking about the royal palace of Babylon. The king spoke, saying, 'Is not this great Babylon, that I have built for a royal dwelling by my mighty power and for the honor of my majesty?' While the word was still in the king's mouth, a voice fell from heaven: 'King Nebuchadnezzar, to you it is spoken: the kingdom has departed from you!'"

Immediately, Nebuchadnezzar went mad. In just a matter of minutes, he went from walking amid the company of his servants in the royal palace to crawling on all fours with the beasts of the field. The Scriptures say that "he was driven from men and ate grass like oxen; his body was wet with the dew of heaven till his hair had grown like eagles' feathers and his nails like birds' claws" (Daniel 4:33). He became quite a sight! And he remained that way for seven long years.

Although we may not be mighty kings like Nebuchad nezzar, we can still carry his same attitude. We may think, *I don't need God. My life is very comfortable. Look at the business I have established. Look at the family I have raised. Look at the money I have made.* What is it going to take to bring us to our senses? When will we realize that the hearts that pump blood into our bodies right now beat by the grace of God? that the breath we draw into our lungs is a gift from God? that the hands we work with and the brains we think with are gifts from God?

For Nebuchadnezzar it took a major touch from God. After he had been out in the field for a while, he may have thought, *This is insanity. I don't want to stay this way. I desperately need the help of the true God.* Then he lifted up his eyes to heaven and called on God. And God extended his mercy to him: "At the end of the time I, Nebuchadnezzar, lifted my eyes to heaven, and my understanding returned to me; and I blessed the Most High and praised and honored Him who lives forever: For His dominion is an everlasting dominion, and His kingdom is from generation to generation" (Daniel 4:34). And look at the final verse in this chapter: "Now I, Nebuchadnezzar, praise and extol and honor the King of heaven, all of whose works are truth, and His ways justice. And those who walk in pride He is able to put down" (Daniel 4:37).

Before, he was always acknowledging the mighty works of the God of Daniel and the Israelites. Now, however, he was acknowledging God as his own personal Lord and King. Before, he had turned to others when he had questions of a spiritual nature. Finally, he realized the importance of going directly to God for help in his time of need.

A. W. Tozer, in his book *That Incredible Christian*, says, "To accept Christ is to form an attachment to the person of our Lord Jesus Christ altogether unique in human experience. The attachment is intellectual, volitional, and emotional."[1]

When King Nebuchadnezzar came to "the end of himself," he finally made that *complete* surrender to God. It wasn't just an intellectual exercise. It wasn't just an emotional experience. It was a sincere, wholehearted commitment to the one true God.

Interestingly, Nebuchadnezzar only lived one year after God restored him to his kingdom. And he used that year to write this wonderful testimony found in Daniel 4. Isn't it a good thing he didn't wait another year to get right with God? Nebuchadnezzar threw most of his life away. But, thank God, in the end he came to his senses.

Are you throwing your life away right now? Do you know God in a personal way? Or have you only paid lip service to the Lord, refusing to completely surrender your life to him. Maybe things are going reasonably well for you. You are not in major trouble at this moment. Then again, maybe the bottom has dropped out. Crisis has hit. You are addicted to drugs or alcohol, or you are in some mess. God offers His forgiveness to you. He offers His hand to you. And if you will call upon Him, He will forgive you.

I urge you not to put this off. The Bible says, "He who is

often rebuked, and hardens his neck, will suddenly be destroyed, and that without remedy" (Proverbs 29:1). In other words, every time you are exposed to the truth of God's Word and you say, "Not now, maybe later," or "Another time perhaps," your heart gets a little harder. The problem is not that God will not forgive you. It's that you do not want to be forgiven. The problem is not that God will not speak to you. It's that you are not able to hear Him because your heart is so callous and tough. That is the danger of putting it off. If you have fallen away from the Lord and your relationship with Him is less than it should be, come back to Him before you heart grows irreparably hard.

There are a lot of fair-weather followers today who fill the pews of churches. Some are nothing more than thrill seekers looking for a spiritual experience. Others come simply to appease their conscience for the way they live the rest of the week. But then there are those who really want to know who God is. They really want to know what His Word says. They want to obey it. It is their desire in life to really learn more about Jesus Christ.

One of the easiest ways to distance yourself from God is to hold on to certain areas of your life that you are afraid of giving over to Him. You cannot serve two masters. God wants to be Lord of your life. It is not enough to work God into your life and plans. Instead, you need to allow God to work in you. When you allow that to happen, God will change your life, giving you new direction and power to live the way He wants you to live.

A FAILURE TO
MOVE FORWARD

*Anyone who lives on milk, being still an infant, is not acquainted
with the teaching about righteousness.*
    HEBREWS 5:13, NIV

Recently, I learned the story of a young woman named Brenda.
She was raised to believe there was no such thing as hell. It
wasn't until she met a group of satanists that she realized the
reality of evil, judgment, and eternity. Like so many people, it
was coming face-to-face with evil that awakened her to the
reality and goodness of God.

Brenda's life had been empty until one day someone
shared the gospel with her. It had such an impact on her that
she immediately took off from work and spent all her time
studying the book of Psalms.

"I remember feeling as though I was being opened up," she
recalls. "Years of feelings surfaced as I read my own heart. I had
an incredible sense of being able to identify with David's heart
as my desire to cry out for the Lord increased."

But after three years of going to church and telling others
about Jesus, Brenda slipped back into her old lifestyle again.
Without even thinking about it, she allowed herself to get
reinvolved in every form of sin from which she had been delivered. It wasn't until four years later that Brenda allowed herself
to reexamine where her life was taking her. She sensed her
brother needed a relationship with Jesus, yet who was she—a

backslidden Christian—to introduce him to the Lord? She tried anyway.

Her brother listened. He said he needed to find a church. Brenda helped him find one. He listened and left with a Bible. After reading a little, he tried to approach God, but he really didn't know how. Initially, he thought he felt some kind of peace, but a voice kept telling him he wasn't worthy of living. Her brother misinterpreted this voice as coming from God. He tried to kill himself by slashing his wrists and stabbing himself in the chest several times.

"I remember feeling such a loss when I had nothing to share with him," Brenda recalls. The experience reminded her of the love and peace she had experienced years before when she was in fellowship with God. Since she had walked away, life had become empty and confusing. The next Sunday she went back to church.

"As I walked in and heard the worship, I was bathed in the presence of the Lord and felt my return was most welcome," she said. "I came to realize that I was like the one of the ninety-nine sheep that had gone astray. I feel so thankful that the Lord brought me back into the fold. I was so grateful for the second chance."

A Spiritual Plateau

I remember, as a young Christian, asking Chuck Smith, the founder of Calvary Chapel, "Chuck, how long have you been a Christian?" He told me it had been around twenty-five years.

I thought, *Wow, twenty-five years! After we have been believers that long we must be on the level of the apostles or something!* Surely after that much time of walking with the Lord, there must be some kind of spiritual plateau we reach—some kind of elevated state where we would somehow be above temptation and all of the problems that many younger Christians face.

Now I have been a Christian for more than twenty-five years. I have been a Christian for longer than I was an unbeliever. And let me say that I have never once in any way regretted my decision to follow Jesus Christ! But I can tell you from experience that there is no safe haven from temptation. Everyone is capable of failing—backsliding. On this earth there is no such thing as a superspiritual state where we no longer grapple with temptation's pull. We never get above it all. The Christian life is one of constant growth.

Remember this: The moment we cease to move forward in our Christian walk is the moment we begin backsliding. For many, *backsliding* is a harsh word. When we think of a backslider, we imagine people who have really gone deep into sin. Their lives are in the pit. Criminals, losers, troublemakers. But we can be regular churchgoers trying to do all the right things and still be backsliders. It's really a measurement of what is in our hearts.

God has a lot to say to backsliders. In Jeremiah 2:19, He says, "Your wickedness will punish you; your backsliding will rebuke you. Consider then and realize how evil and bitter it is for you when you forsake the Lord your God and have no awe of me" (NIV). We are told in Proverbs 14:14, "The backslider in heart will be filled with his own ways." And then Jeremiah 3:22 says, " 'Return, faithless people; I will cure you of backsliding.' 'Yes, we will come to you, for you are the Lord our God' " (NIV).

Although some would agree that they are not as active spiritually as they should be, and many would say they are not as close to the Lord as they would like to be, most of us don't think of ourselves as backsliders. The word has such power—it's so dramatic. I think we need to be careful, however, not to think that just because we're not living in gross sin that somehow we haven't backslidden or that we're not at least on the road to it. Christians need to be constantly on guard about their spiritual state. We are all exposed to the temptations of this alluring world. We are all susceptible to falling away, especially in these times.

The Bible warns that in the last days there will come an "apostasy." That word simply means that there will be many who fall away. The Bible says, in 1 Timothy 4:1, "Some will depart from the faith, giving heed to deceiving spirits and doctrines of demons."

Which Way Are We Going?

If we're not moving toward God, we're moving away from Him. It's like parking a car on a hill and putting it in neutral. Which way are you going to go? Up or down? In the same way, if I put my Christian life in neutral—if I stop seeking to learn and grow as a believer—I will naturally go the wrong way. I will go backward. I will go down.

I read about a sign at the end of a road near an airport runway. It said, "Keep moving. If you stop, you are in danger and a danger to those who are flying." You could apply the same principle to the Christian life. Keep moving. If you stop, you are in danger and a danger to others. We have a natural tendency to slip back into our old sinful ways. I have a natural tendency to do what's wrong. But then I have a supernatural tendency to do what's right.

We can compare our tendencies to a flower and a weed. A weed is like our old nature—that part of us that doesn't want to obey God. The flower is like our new nature. My wife loves to plant flowers. She tends them and cares for them. She puts snail repellent down, picks any weeds that get even remotely close, fertilizes them, and watches over them. But I've noticed a rather strange phenomenon. In the same time it takes for that beautiful little flower to grow two inches, a new weed bursts through some crack in the street and grows about eighteen feet high! How much nurturing did the weed need? None.

Like the fragile flower, the new nature needs nurturing. It needs encouraging. As believers we need to do the things that build us up spiritually. The old nature, however, needs little or no encouragement. If we neglect spiritual growth, we will be shocked by how quickly and easily we can be pulled in the wrong direction.

Most people think, *Well, I'm not doing anything that bad. I'm not in prison. I'm working hard to support my family. I'm not hurting anyone.* That's not the issue. Are you doing the good things? The Christian life is not about just ceasing to do what is wrong; it's about engaging in what is right. The Christian life is not just about obeying commandments; it's about wanting to please the Lord—wanting to grow, trying to become more like Him.

I would never fall away, some of us think. *I would never backslide. I love God too much. My devotion is too deep.* Watch out, friend! Those sound like famous last words to me. The Bible says, "Let him who thinks he stands take heed lest he fall" (1 Corinthians 10:12). The Bible also says, "Pride goes before destruction, and a haughty spirit before a fall" (Proverbs 16:18). It is often the seemingly strong person who is most vulnerable. The prideful person trusts himself. The person who recognizes his own weaknesses is more likely to be totally dependent on God for strength.

Understanding Our Weaknesses

After three years of walking with Jesus, Simon Peter thought that he would never let the Lord down, under any circumstances. As a disciple, handpicked by Jesus Himself, he honestly thought that he was above stumbling spiritually. Others might fall, but not him. He was above it all—or so he thought. Of course, he fell—and he fell big.

The story of Peter's downfall describes a man who didn't understand his own weakness. It's one of the most famous failure stories in history. But it's not only the story of failure—it's also the story of God's forgiveness and restoration. It's the story of how God generously gives all of us second chances.

Remember that when Jesus called Peter, He knew what He was doing. He knew what Peter was made of. Do you realize that your shortcomings and failures come as no surprise to God? God is omniscient, which means He knows everything about you. For as David said in Psalm 139:1-3, "O Lord, You have searched me and known me. You know my sitting down and my rising up; You understand my thought afar off. You comprehend my path and my lying down, and are acquainted with all my ways." Jesus Christ knows us better than we know ourselves. So it comes as no surprise to Him when we fail. Likewise, He knew that Peter would fail. He predicted it, much to Peter's disbelief.

Jesus loved this man just as He loves us. And He gave him a second chance. Peter's failure stands as a warning to even the most mature believer. For three years Peter had spent every waking moment of his life in the presence of God Incarnate. He was there when Jesus fed the multitudes with the loaves and fishes. He was there when Jesus delivered the greatest message ever spoken, the Sermon on the Mount. He was there when Lazarus was resurrected from the dead after being dead for four days. He was there when Jesus defied natural law and walked on the water. In fact, for a few moments, Peter had even joined Him out on the lake.

He had had every spiritual privilege one could hope for in life. He had witnessed many dramatic miracles. And he had faithfully followed Jesus, the greatest conceivable example of a godly life. Yet he still fell.

Setting the Stage

Before we examine the reasons for Peter's fall, let's recall the setting. The disciples were in the upper room about to receive the Last Supper—the final meal that Jesus would eat with them. Jesus had sent Peter and John to set up the room and to make preparations for the Passover. Finally, Jesus and the other disciples arrived.

Normally, in that culture, a servant would have been waiting at the door to wash the feet of the guests. It was a customary gesture. People wore open-toed sandals, and the roads in Israel were dusty. Washing the feet of guests was common. But as the disciples arrived, no one washed anyone's feet. Why? Most likely because a pecking order, or hierarchy, had emerged among the disciples. On more than one occasion they had argued about who would be greatest in the kingdom. Because no one wanted to appear subservient to the others, nobody dared to humble himself and wash the others' feet. They all walked in and took their seats at the table.

When we think of the Last Supper, we envision a long table with everyone sitting on one side, as if they were posing for a photo. That's how the great Renaissance painter Leonardo de Vinci portrayed it. With all due respect to Leonardo, I seriously doubt that's the way it was. In reality, they didn't use long tables or high-backed chairs during this era. The table was probably round and low to the ground. The men would have sat on cushions rather than chairs. Some of them may have even been in a semi-reclined position.

The meal included a long, drawn-out ritual. It was not something that took place in twenty minutes with people wolfing down their food and calling for the check. In the first century the evening meal was the main event—a time of discussion, interaction, and fellowship. It would sometimes go on for hours.

As the disciples were waiting for the meal to begin, Jesus

did something completely unexpected. He took off His outer garment. Then He reached over and picked up a basin of water, got down on His hands and knees, and personally began to wash the disciples' feet, one by one.

This must have amazed and humbled the disciples as they watched the Master do the work normally reserved for a servant. But He was modeling something extremely important to men who would be leaders one day. They had to learn to serve and do it willingly and gladly.

What I find especially amazing is the fact that He washed everyone's feet, including those of the man who within minutes would betray and abandon Him, Judas Iscariot. If I had been there, I would not have washed this man's feet. I would have dumped the basin of water on him, picked him up by the scruff of the neck, and thrown him right out the window! But Jesus, always loving, always giving opportunities to repent, washed the feet of Judas along with the others.

As Jesus made the rounds, He came to Simon Peter. Peter protested (loudly, no doubt), "My feet shall not be washed by you." Jesus replied, "If I do not wash you, you have no part with Me." Peter, quickly reconsidering, shot back, "Well, don't just wash my feet. Wash my hands and head, too." Essentially he was saying, "Give me a bath, Lord." I imagine Jesus might have chuckled a little at that suggestion. It was classic Peter, always speaking his mind.

Later, as the disciples sat, Jesus turned to Simon Peter and said something that must have shocked him to the core: "Simon, Simon! Indeed, Satan has asked for you, that he may sift you as wheat. But I have prayed for you, that your faith should not fail; and when you have returned to Me, strengthen your brethren" (Luke 22:31-32). Presumably, Peter fixated on the word *return*. You can imagine him thinking, *What do you mean return to you? I'm not going anywhere*. He protested and blurted out, "Lord, I am ready to go with You, both to prison and to death" (Luke 22:33). Jesus, hearing these words, corrected his self-confident disciple by saying, "I tell you, Peter, the rooster shall not crow this day before you will deny three times that you know Me" (Luke 22:34).

Denying the Denial

Can you imagine if you were in the upper room with Jesus and the disciples and He said this to you? There you are among your closest friends, men you have spent three years of your life with. And there sits before you the One for whom you would do anything. Your admiration for Him knows no bounds. Your heart burns with a love for and devotion to this man, who is actually God in human form. You literally worship Him, and so you should.

You might have been looking around at the others and sizing them up. *I don't like this Thomas character, always with the questions. He just doesn't seem that loyal to me. Then there's John. He really irritates me at times, too. Why is he always sitting so close to Jesus, leaning his head on His chest and all? Doesn't Jesus see what a self-seeking flatterer he is?*

Then you might have looked over at Judas and thought, *Now that Judas is a real stand-up guy. I like the way he spoke up for the poor the other day when that woman was wasting that expensive perfume on Jesus.*

Appearances can be deceiving, can't they? Things are not always as they seem. Peter could have been thinking, *I don't know about the rest of these guys, but Jesus has no more loyal follower in this room than I am. I'd do anything for Him. I'd even die for Him! Why I'd—*

Suddenly, his thoughts are interrupted by the voice of Jesus. With those piercing eyes locked on Peter's, He says, "Satan has been asking for you." Can you imagine how terrifying that would be? A more literal rendering of that verse from the Greek would be, "Satan has been asking excessively for you by name, that you would be taken out of the care and keeping of God."

We often say, "The devil tempted me the other day. Satan has really been giving me a hard time lately." I would suggest to you that most of us have probably never actually been tempted by the devil himself. Understand what I am saying. The devil has many demonic forces to do his bidding. But the devil himself can only be in one place at a time. He is not omnipresent like God. He is not able to be everywhere at once. You would have to be a pretty big fish for the devil himself to be asking for you by name! The point of this story is that the devil, the prince of the power of the air, the god of this world, the very kingpin of evil, was saying, "I want *Peter*."

Let's not miss something significant here. Satan had to ask; he couldn't just take Peter down at will. I'm sure he would have if it had been possible. He couldn't take Peter down at will, and he can't take us down at will if we have committed our lives to Jesus Christ. I hear some people say, "The devil pulled me down the other day. I was just minding my own business, walking with the Lord, and the devil just grabbed me." That is not possible if we are children of God. The devil can't just "get us." We are under God's protection. In essence, we have invisible signs hanging around our necks that say Under New Management.

That's not to say we won't be tempted. It doesn't mean that Satan's minions will not try to hassle us. But he cannot just pick us off at will. He has to ask permission of Jesus Christ. So the next time the enemy comes knocking at the door of your life, just say, "Lord, would You mind getting that?" Flee temptation, and don't leave a forwarding address!

Jesus told Peter, "Satan has been asking that you be taken out of God's care and protection. But I have prayed that your faith not fail." Think about that. If we knew that Jesus was in the same room praying for us specifically by name, wouldn't that encourage us? Wouldn't it give us strength? If you are a Christian, I have some good news! Jesus Christ is praying for you right now. In Hebrews 7:25 the Bible says, "He is able to save completely those who come to God through him, because he always lives to intercede for them" (NIV). Just as surely as Jesus was standing in the gap for Peter, He is standing there for you. You are not alone.

Peter considered what Jesus told him. He probably thought, *This is crazy. There is no way I would fail the Lord.* This prompted him to blurt out self-confidently, "Lord, I am ready to go with you to prison and to death" (Luke 22:33, NIV). Matthew 26:33 tells us that he added, "Even if all are made to stumble because of You, I will never be made to stumble."

Watch out for people who make themselves look good at others' expense—people who will cut down others and then boast about how great they are. That's essentially what Peter did: "If all deny you, I, Peter the Rock (remember, Lord, You gave me that new name), will never let You down. Matthew, James, and John—I don't know what they may do. But as for me, I will never deny You."

Jesus says, "Well, as a matter of fact, Peter, you will deny Me three times."

No, Peter thought, *it's not possible.*

But it was possible. It is possible for all of us. Consequently, we must learn the steps that could lead us down the wrong path in order to avoid them. Stay tuned!

SEVEN STEPS TO
SPIRITUAL FAILURE

Let him who thinks he stands take heed lest he fall.
    1 CORINTHIANS 10:12

I received a letter that really touched my heart from a young
woman in an Oregon prison. Let's call her Kris. It was her first
time in prison. She's out now. She had to serve only sixty days.
But, as she explained, "That was enough."

> The reason I'm writing to you is because—twenty years
> ago—my parents used to force me to come to church (your
> church). I've always been religious. But the other morning
> I committed my life to the Lord. I was up all night crying
> over a broken marriage and my past. The Lord answered
> my prayers by saying, "Commit yourself to me." He came
> to me that morning and made my tears turn into smiles
> and laughs. About that time your voice came over the
> radio. You have this very distinctive voice. I remembered
> that from eighteen to twenty years ago when I was seven
> or eight years old going to your church. I heard your
> message over the air. I don't know why I'm writing to
> you—I guess for your prayers. I get out in thirty days, and I
> don't want to go back to my old ways. I want to be strong
> in the Lord. So maybe you could pray for me.

I do pray for her as well as for those out there facing similar situations. We all need help in our walk with God, and here is a young woman who knows she has made mistakes and is trying to get right with God. What led to her failure?

Let's explore seven downward steps, based on Peter's experience, that lead to the pit of spiritual failure.

1. *Self-Confidence.* The first step is found in Luke 22:33 where Peter said, "Lord, I am ready to go with You, both to prison and to death." His first step to spiritual failure and denial was self-confidence. In speaking these words, Peter not only revealed an unfounded pride in himself, he also directly contradicted his Lord's prediction. He was saying, "Jesus, You're wrong. I don't know what the problem is, but Lord, You have got this one wrong." Obviously, if Jesus said it, Peter should have admitted, "I don't understand how I can do that, but if You say it, I know it will happen."

Mark tells us that Peter repeatedly insisted on his loyalty. On the surface this almost sounds somewhat commendable. But looked at another way, we can and should see it for what it was—wrong and sinful. He was full of himself—proud, self-confident. That was his first mistake.

2. *Prayerlessness.* In Luke 22:39-46 we read these words:

Coming out, He went to the Mount of Olives, as He was accustomed, and His disciples also followed Him. When He came to the place, He said to them [Peter, James, and John], "Pray that you may not enter into temptation."

And He was withdrawn from them about a stone's throw, and He knelt down and prayed, saying, "Father, if it is Your will, take this cup away from Me; nevertheless not My will, but Yours, be done." Then an angel appeared to Him from heaven, strengthening Him. And being in agony, He prayed more earnestly. Then His sweat became like great drops of blood falling down to the ground.

When He rose up from prayer, and had come to His disciples, He found them sleeping from sorrow. Then He said to them, "Why do you sleep? Rise and pray, lest you enter into temptation."

Peter's prayerlessness was, no doubt, a direct result of his self-confidence. Jesus had specifically instructed him to pray. But what did he do? He slept. Granted, deep sorrow prompted it, but still he slept. Peter rarely seemed to get it right.

Later, when the soldiers came to arrest Jesus in the Garden of Gethsemane, Peter pulled out a sword and started swinging away. In the process, he severed the ear of the servant of the high priest standing nearby.

Jesus turned to Peter and said, "Put that sword away. What are you doing? Don't you think that I could ask My Father right now and twelve legions of angels would come and deliver me?" So when he should have been watching, he was sleeping. And when he should have been trusting, he was fighting! Peter's lack of prayer reminds us that there are sins of omission as well as sins of commission.

I heard about a Sunday school worker who was teaching her first grade class. Her subject of the day was sin. She wanted the kids to know about the different types of sin that can be committed. So she asked the students, "Does anyone know what sins of commission are?"

A little girl answered, "That's when you do something your mommy told you not to do."

"Very good!" the teacher said. "Now, can anyone tell me what a sin of omission might be?"

A little boy was frantically waving his hand, and she called on him. He proudly announced, "Those are all the sins you're supposed to commit but haven't got around to yet!"

That's how a lot of Christians act today. We think it's only a matter of time until we commit certain sins. Some of us will say, "This temptation to have sex before marriage is too powerful!" Or, "This peer pressure to drink and do drugs is hard to resist! I'm going to cave in any time now! I don't know how long I'll be able to hold out!"

But sins can be resisted! We don't have to be victims. Not only can we resist sin as Christians, we can grow stronger spiritually every day. But we can't do it with our own strength!

Peter's sin of omission was failing to pray when instructed to do so by Jesus Himself. So sin is not just doing the wrong things; it is failing to do the right ones, too.

Did Jesus say, "Men ought to pray whenever they are in a good mood?" I don't think so. He said, "Men always ought to pray and not lose heart" (Luke 18:1). The Bible says, "Pray without ceasing . . . for this is the will of God in Christ Jesus for you" (1 Thessalonians 5:17-18). Clearly God is saying that prayer should be an important and regular part of our lives.

If I say no to God's instruction, that is a sin. And that is what happened to Peter.

3. *Following at a distance.* Peter's third step down was following Jesus at a distance. Luke 22:54 says, "Having arrested Him, they led Him and brought Him into the high priest's house. But Peter followed at a distance." What does that mean? Being a Christian means getting as close to God as we can. But Peter was following at a distance, literally, in this case.

Do you know people like that? They show up in church occasionally. On one hand, they want to keep one foot in it, so to speak. On the other hand, they don't want to make that total commitment. This distance from the Lord in closeness and fellowship is always at the foundation of all spiritual regression and failure.

I don't know about you, but I don't like jumping into cold water. When I'm at the beach or at a lake and the water's cold,

I know the best way to get in is to just jump in. Get it over with, and then you feel great. But getting in slowly is the worst possible way.

One overcast day I was at the beach with my son Jonathan. The water was icy cold, but I wanted to swim with him. It wasn't quite deep enough for me to dive in yet, so I slowly (and, I might add, miserably) made my way into the water. First, I got my feet wet . . . then my ankles . . . then up to my knees. I wasn't completely dry or wet. I was at that unhappy, in-between stage where even a stray drop of freezing water is torturous.

That is how many of us are spiritually. We don't want to take the plunge and walk as closely to God as possible. Then again, we don't want to stay on the shore either. But we must decide; we can't have it both ways.

Many people today are simply following Jesus Christ at a distance. Show me a marriage that is falling apart, and I will show you a man and a woman who have lost the romance in their relationship. But as long as they are staying close, as long as they are doing the things that keep a marriage strong and healthy, they will not only survive but flourish. As soon as that relationship grows cold, they will start looking around for another one. In the same way, when we lose our closeness with the Lord in fellowship, it's only a matter of time until we look for something or someone else to take His place. The best antidote against backsliding is a close and intimate walk with Christ that is maintained on a daily basis.

4. *Consorting with the enemy.* The fourth step down for this self-confident disciple took place when he warmed himself at the enemy's fire. But what *led* Peter to the fireside is worth noting. John's account of this story gives us a unique insight not found in the other Gospels:

"Simon Peter and another disciple were following Jesus. Because this disciple was known to the high priest, he went with Jesus into the high priest's courtyard, but Peter had to wait outside at the door. The other disciple, who was known to the high priest, came back, spoke to the girl on duty there and brought Peter in" (John 18:15-16, NIV).

From this account we see that John apparently knew the high priest personally and was able to walk right into his quarters and witness the cross-examination of Jesus. After being let in at the door, Peter presumably could have joined him, but he didn't.

5. *Denying the Lord.* The striking thing about this account is that when John came out and asked the maid to let Peter in, she asked Peter, "You are not also one of this Man's disciples, are you?" (John 18:17).

He responded, "I am not." He had no reason at all to deny his connection to Jesus. At that point he was in no danger. John also was a disciple, and through this whole account he had never been hassled. If Peter had just told the truth, he could have witnessed what John saw. And he would never have been put in a position to deny the Lord. But Peter foolishly determined to do it his way. That is what got him into trouble. He lied and then soon lied again to cover up for himself. This single lie swept him into a set of circumstances he could not believe.

6. *Denying the Lord again.* Now Peter was standing and warming himself by the enemy's fire. No doubt his heart was pounding, and his blood ran cold from what he had just done. Suddenly, he was recognized again!

Another said, "You are not also one of His disciples, are you?" (John 18:25).

He denied it, saying, "I am not!"

This was his second denial. You would think he would have remembered the words of the Lord about this. But who thinks logically when he is caught in the riptide of sin? We think we can control our slide into sin and put on the brakes at any time we choose.

It's those famous last words. The person who has success-fully stayed on a diet for weeks says, "I'll have just one bite." The person who knows his vulnerability to the power of alcohol justifies tasting it by saying, "I'll stop after one drink." The girl who gets herself into a compromising situation with some guy, knowing the temptation will surely strike, says, "I'll just tell him I'm not that kind of girl."

There was Peter, warming himself at the enemy's fire. *This can't hurt*, he probably thought. But he was in the wrong place, with the wrong people, about to do the wrong thing.

People with whom we associate are going to have an influence on our lives. Scripture warns us, "Do not be misled: 'Bad company corrupts good character' " (1 Corinthians 15:33, NIV). And again, "Flee the evil desires of youth, and pursue righ-teousness, faith, love and peace, along with those who call on the Lord out of a pure heart" (2 Timothy 2:22, NIV).

Be careful whom you choose as your close friends. Look for godly people. Look for people who will encourage you, people who will build you up spiritually.

Shortly after I became a believer, I was in no-man's-land for a couple of weeks. I had just become a Christian. I knew that Jesus Christ was real. When I tried to hang out with my old friends, I immediately knew that their lifestyle was no longer for me. The appeal was completely gone.

For a short period of time I tried to be what you might call a "solo Christian." It was going to be just me and God. That's all I thought I needed. But I found out I needed more. We all do. We can't make it on our own. So we can't treat fellowship with other believers as an optional part of our faith. The Bible says, "Not forsaking the assembling of ourselves together, as is the manner of some, but exhorting one another, and so much the more as you see the Day approaching" (Hebrews 10:25).

Peter was really in a vulnerable position at that point.

Already two denials had taken place. It was time to hightail it out of there. After the second denial, Mark tells us that Peter went out to the porch. He probably walked out slowly so no one would think he was about to run away. An hour went by before the third denial. Peter had an hour to come to his senses and say to himself, *Jesus said I would deny Him three times. I have already denied Him twice. Maybe I shouldn't be here.* But no, Peter stayed. Why? Because his Lord was not far away. Jesus was in there being examined, being tried on bogus, trumped-up charges. Part of Peter wanted to be near Jesus. Part of him wanted to get away. He was in spiritual conflict. Have you ever felt that way? You know what is right, but you struggle to do it.

7. *Total denial.* Last step and third denial. Someone else recognized Peter as a follower of Jesus. And Matthew's account says, "He began to curse and swear, saying, 'I do not know the Man!' " (Matthew 26:74).

This phrase "curse and swear" is not referring to profanity per se. It does not mean that Peter "swore like a sailor" (though he was one, of sorts). The phrase that he used pronounced death on himself at the hand of God if he were lying. It is, perhaps, the most serious form of taking the Lord's name in vain. Peter said, in essence, "May God kill and damn me if I am not speaking the truth." Can you imagine that? He had sunk lower than he ever thought possible.

How did Peter sink so low? A series of steps. It didn't happen in the blink of an eye. It never does. But it started with self-confidence, prayerlessness, following at a distance, warming himself at the enemy's fire, denying Jesus, then denying Him again, and, finally, being so blinded that he swore an oath of total denial and took the Lord's name in vain. He had lost all sense of reality, all perspective, all awareness of God.

Then, in one of the most powerful verses in the Bible, we are told, "The Lord turned and looked at Peter. Then Peter remembered the word of the Lord, how He had said to him, 'Before the rooster crows, you will deny Me three times' " (Luke 22:61).

What a moment that must have been. I have often tried to imagine the expression on Jesus' face when His eyes met those of His fallen disciple. How do you think the Lord looked at Peter? Was it a look of hatred? A look of complete disgust? Did tears roll out of His eyes? I can't say with certainty how Jesus looked at Peter. But knowing Jesus, I think it was a look of deep compassion—a look of love, a look of forgiveness. Why? Because Jesus had known the denial was coming. He also knew that Peter would come back to Him. I'm sure Peter remembered that look that said, "Peter, I still love you." I think that's why Peter went out and wept bitterly.

Keep in mind that, at this point, the disciples didn't under stand that Jesus was going to die and be resurrected. In fact, when Jesus brought up the subject of His crucifixion, it was Peter who rebuked Him and said, "Lord, this cannot happen! This is definitely a bad idea!" When Jesus was taken a short time later to be crucified, they watched in horror as the life drained out of His body. They watched Him say "It is finished" and then die. They probably thought, *It's finished, all right. We're finished. Our lives have been wasted. There is no hope.*

Somehow they had missed the many times when Jesus had spoken of His resurrection from the dead. That's why it came as a great surprise to the disciples when the Lord did indeed arise.

When Jesus arose, this message was delivered to His defeated disciple: "Go, tell His disciples—and Peter—that He is going before you into Galilee; there you will see Him, as He said to you" (Mark 16:7).

Isn't that amazing? Why do you think the Lord threw in Peter's name? I think it was because He knew Peter was hurting. He knew it was Peter who most needed reassurance. In time Peter was forgiven by the Lord, and he was restored. Jesus gave him a second chance, which I will describe later.

Like Peter, no matter what you have done, Jesus will forgive you, too. But you must be willing to be forgiven.

During that long night for the Lord and Peter, two men passed through the doorway into the darkness of the city. One man turned and walked into the bitterness of eternal remorse. He betrayed the Lord for thirty pieces of silver. His name was Judas Iscariot. He went out and hanged himself. The other man turned and walked into the open arms of God. His name was Simon Peter. Yes, he had failed. Yes, he wept bitterly. But he came back to the Lord.

We're all going to fail God at times in our lives. We're all going to sin. To deny that reality is foolish. John even says, "If we say that we have no sin, we deceive ourselves, and the truth is not in us" (1 John 1:8). But then he makes provision for those times of lapse: "My dear children, I write this to you so that you will not sin. But if anybody does sin, we have one who speaks to the Father in our defense—Jesus Christ, the Righteous One. He is the atoning sacrifice for our sins, and not only for ours but also for the sins of the whole world" (1 John 2:1-2, NIV).

The question is not whether I'm going to fail. The question is *where* and *when*. And then, more important, what am I going to do with my failure? Will I learn a valuable life lesson from it? Will I want to avoid what led me to that situation in the future? Will I warn others if I see them falling into the same potential trap? If so, then I have failed forward—I've learned from my mistakes. I learned the hard way, granted, but I have learned.

Or will I just go out and do the same stupid things that led to my fall again and again and then scratch my head in wonder, asking, "How did this happen to me again?" If so, I have learned nothing. I have failed backward. It's my choice. And it's yours. Make the right decision. Fail forward!

YOU CAN HAVE A SECOND ChANCE

Part 3

SECOND CHANCES
FOR SHATTERED LIVES

"Then neither do I condemn you," Jesus declared. "Go now
and leave your life of sin."
  JOHN 8:11, NIV

At the end of 1995 I received a moving letter from a man in Illinois
who had devoted his life to Christ, had gone to church every week
for several years, and had even become a Bible teacher because of
his commitment to his faith. But this man—let's call him Paul—
stumbled spiritually toward the end of 1992. He started to wander
from the Lord and slowly, perhaps imperceptibly at first, began to
fall back into his old lifestyle.

"I met a woman," Paul recalls, "and put my love for her
above my love for Christ. At that time it seemed to be the most
wonderful and joyous time of my life. I began to fall into my old
sinful nature of alcohol abuse and drugs along with my lust for
money and sex."

Paul and his girlfriend slept together. They partied. And
Paul forgot about God.

"Our relationship seemed to be the most important thing
in our lives. We had no regard for Christ as we drifted further
into sin and worldly behavior," he recalled.

Then one night in 1993, Paul and his girlfriend were out for
a night of drinking and socializing. They drove from one party to
another. The plan was to spend the night at the home of some
friends. But Paul was tired, so his girlfriend offered to drive.

"Falling asleep, I awoke to the sounds of screeching brakes and shattering glass," Paul remembers. "Immediately I lost consciousness."

In the emergency room Paul learned that his girlfriend had been killed. At a memorial service for her, a clergyman read Psalm 23:

The Lord is my shepherd; I shall not want.
He makes me to lie down in green pastures;
He leads me beside the still waters.
He restores my soul;
He leads me in the paths of righteousness for His name's sake.

Yea, though I walk through the valley of the shadow of death,
I will fear no evil;
For You are with me;
Your rod and Your staff, they comfort me.

You prepare a table before me in the presence of my enemies;
You anoint my head with oil;
My cup runs over.
Surely goodness and mercy shall follow me
All the days of my life;
And I will dwell in the house of the Lord
Forever.

Rather than being comforted by this Scripture, Paul was tormented by it. Why? Because he wasn't sure about his girlfriend's relationship with the Lord and her eternal fate. Worse yet, he realized he had not fulfilled his obligation before God to share the gospel with her, much less live it himself.

"Instead, I had been selfish and sinful," Paul wrote. "For a long time I struggled and grieved over my girlfriend's death, and then I justified it by saying it was God's time for her and ratio-nalizing that she was happier now. I now realize it was a consequence of our sin and our disobedience to God—not God's vengeance, as many people would believe."

Toward the end of 1995—more than two and a half years after his girlfriend's death—Paul began listening to my radio program. He credits it with leading him to the recommitment of his life to the Lord.

Nature of the Beast

You don't have to be a powerful and famous person like King Nebuchadnezzar or an apostle like Peter to get second chances from God. Some of the best second-chance stories I have ever heard are about ordinary people, like Paul, caught up in ordinary human circumstances that turn tragic because of sin.

Have you ever been caught in the act of doing something wrong? One day back when my son Jonathan was nine, I found him watching television. That wasn't necessarily a bad thing, but the rule in our house was that he couldn't watch any TV or play any video games until he had finished his schoolwork. Well, I'd caught him in the act. I peeked in his room, and there he was in front of the blue glow of the TV.

He looked at me with a guilty expression and spun off a classic excuse: "I couldn't resist myself."

To be honest, I thought it was kind of cute, the way he put it. He didn't say, "I couldn't resist temptation." Instead, he stam-mered, "I couldn't resist myself."

This incident with Jonathan reminds me of the fable of the scorpion and the turtle. As you may know, scorpions can't swim. One day a scorpion that wanted to cross a pond found a turtle and asked if he would give him a lift across.

The turtle exclaimed, "Are you joking? You'll sting me while I'm swimming, and I'll drown."

"My dear turtle," laughed the scorpion, "as you say, if I were to sting you, you would drown, and I'd go down with you. Now where is the logic in that?"

"You've got a point there," agreed the turtle. "Hop on."

The scorpion climbed aboard, and halfway across the river, he carefully aimed his powerful stinger, and with a mighty jolt, stung the turtle with everything he had.

As they both sank to the bottom, the turtle, resigned to his fate, turned to the scorpion and said, "Do you mind if I ask you something? You said there was no logic in your stinging me. Why did you do it?"

"It has nothing to do with logic," the drowning scorpion replied. "It's just my nature."

In a way, that is a very accurate way of defining temptation. When we are tempted and give in to it, we like to place the blame on someone or something else. "The devil made me do it," we say. Or, we insist, "That person trapped me. I'm not responsible." But the fact is, "It's just our nature." Or, as Jonathan Laurie, the great nine-year-old theologian, said, "I couldn't resist myself."

Think back to the Garden of Eden. Remember how Adam was caught in the act?

The Lord said, "Adam, did you eat the forbidden fruit?"

How did Adam respond? "It's the woman you gave me, Lord. She made me do it."

This idea of refusing to accept responsibility for what we have done is nothing new. The Bible says that a man is tempted when he is drawn by his own lusts. We all play a role in our own temptation. Sure, the devil may entice us. Sure, someone may try to trap us. But they will not be successful unless we give in to that temptation. So when my son said, "I couldn't resist myself," he was accurately describing just what temptation is all about.

A book I wrote titled *The Great Compromise* deals more in depth with this subject. You may want to look it over, especially the chapter called "The Snare of Adultery and the Wildfire of Immorality."[1]

Temptation is everywhere—especially sexual temptation. Nowhere is there more inspiration for sexual temptation today than on television. A survey conducted by Louis Harris and Associates found that the three largest networks broadcast more than sixty-five thousand sexual references every year in the prime afternoon and evening hours. That's only the three largest networks! That doesn't include MTV, VH1, the other cable channels, or Fox. The study determined that the average American TV viewer watches fourteen thousand references to sex in the course of a year.

Another survey, conducted in 1996 by the Kaiser Family Foundation, pointed out that TV's so-called "family hour"—8 to 9 P.M.—is loaded with sexual themes and innuendos. According to a 1996 Associated Press article, about 75 percent of family shows contain some kind of sexual content. That's up from 65 percent in 1986 and 43 percent in 1976.

Where do young people get their ideas about sexuality? A survey of teenagers found that the number one source of that information is the media. The second source mentioned was friends and peers. It's no wonder we have so much trouble in this area. Certainly the media do not encourage morality, at least by biblical standards. If anything, the idea of abstinence before marriage and faithfulness afterward is looked at as outdated, puritanical, and even oppressive.

The thinking goes like this: If *you* want to live that way, go ahead, but don't you dare suggest that your choice is the norm. "Everything is to be tolerated and even encouraged," we are told. Not only is immorality dangerous spiritually, it also is dangerous to you physically. You can literally lose your life. One moment of guilty pleasure can lead to a lifetime of regret. Worse, it can lead to the end of your life altogether. AIDS cases among teenagers and adults grew 77 percent between 1995 and 1997. Thousands are infected who have not even been diagnosed yet. Millions are at risk, according to the World Health Organization.

It was hoped that a cure for this deadly virus would have been discovered by now. But no cure is in sight, though countless millions of dollars have been spent to find it. One of the most frightening things about AIDS is the way it lies dormant in your system for a while. You can be sexually immoral today and reap the deadly results ten years from now.

What does our government do to confront this challenge? How are we spending our tax dollars to try to turn the tide of this trend? Are we teaching abstinence? No, that's considered a moral judgment. That's a religious viewpoint, we are told. Instead, our public schools are teaching the *mythology* of safe sex. I emphasize the word *mythology* for good reason. We are told there's something called "safe sex." We are told that condoms are the answer, but condoms have a failure rate of 15 to 36 percent! One study of married couples in which one partner was infected with HIV found that 17 percent of those partners using condoms for protection still caught the virus within a year and a half. That doesn't sound very safe to me.

Imagine yourself on an airplane. As you are taxiing down the runway, the captain makes an announcement: "Hello, ladies and gentlemen. We have been experiencing a few technical difficulties—some problems with the engine. But I have been assured that we are probably going to make it to our destination. There is a 10 percent chance we will not make it." Now if you were given a chance to deplane, would you? How about if the captain said there was a 17 percent chance you would not make it? How many passengers do you think would stay on board? What if he said there is a 36 percent chance you would not make it? Of course, no one in his right mind would stay on that plane. Yet, people will believe in something called safe sex with the potential of contracting the AIDS virus (or countless other diseases).

And that's just the physical risk we take with immorality. What about the emotional risks? There is no condom designed to protect our mind from unwanted memories. There is no condom that can shield our heart from the guilt and shame that follow sin. But my primary concern is what this lifestyle does to us spiritually. It doesn't matter how tough we are. It doesn't matter whether we are men or women.

Think of Samson, for instance—that he-man with a *she* weakness. Here was a man with supernatural physical strength who thought he could handle the temptations of a young woman named Delilah, whose name, by the way, means "delicate." Because of his incredible strength, Samson would go out and single-handedly slaughter a thousand Philistines with nothing more than a large bone in his hand. Naturally, he thought, *What possible harm could this little, delicate woman do to me?*

He toyed around with this temptation as if it were a game. He continued to sin against God. The Lord gave him warning after warning to stop. He continued to play with sin until, ultimately, sin played around with him. When he finally came to his senses and turned to God, it was too late to save his life. He threw it all away for a few moments of guilty pleasure. Satan could not bring him down on the battlefield, so he destroyed him in the bedroom.

The Bible compares sin to fire: "Can a man scoop fire into his lap without his clothes being burned?" (Proverbs 6:27, NIV). The answer is no. If you dabble in sin, it can take over your life and devastate it. Is there an alternative? Yes, there is. If you have fallen, know that there is forgiveness. There are always second chances for those who have failed morally. There are always second chances to put shattered lives back together again.

e i g h t

A SIN FORGIVEN,
A LIFE RESTORED

Neither do I condemn you; go and sin no more.
JOHN 8:11

John 8 includes the story of a woman caught in the act of adultery. Under the law in that culture, the penalty for such a sin was death by stoning. For this woman, what could have potentially been the worst—and last—day of her life turned out to be the best. That's because she encountered Jesus, and He gave her a second chance.

Let's take a closer look at this important second-chance story:

Now early in the morning He came again into the temple, and all the people came to Him; and He sat down and taught them. Then the scribes and Pharisees brought to Him a woman caught in adultery. And when they had set her in the midst, they said to Him, "Teacher, this woman was caught in adultery, in the very act. Now Moses, in the law, commanded us that such should be stoned. But what do You say?" This they said, testing Him, that they might have something of which to accuse Him. But Jesus stooped down and wrote on the ground with His finger, as though He did not hear.

So when they continued asking Him, He raised Himself up and said to them, "He who is without sin

among you, let him throw a stone at her first." And again
He stooped down and wrote on the ground. Then those
who heard it, being convicted by their conscience, went
out one by one, beginning with the oldest even to the last.
And Jesus was left alone, and the woman standing in the
midst. When Jesus had raised Himself up and saw no one
but the woman, He said to her, "Woman, where are those
accusers of yours? Has no one condemned you?"

She said, "No one, Lord."

And Jesus said to her, "Neither do I condemn you; go
and sin no more." (John 8:2-11)

On the evening before this event, we know that Jesus went to
the mountain and spent time in prayer. Meanwhile, the Pharisees and the religious leaders had spent the whole night hatch-
ing this scheme to trap the Lord. You might say that, while Jesus
was communing with heaven, His enemies were communing
with hell. They wanted Jesus Christ eliminated. He was bad for
their business. Instead of playing their religious game and
taking advantage of the people in every way, He came and
demonstrated the love and Word of God to them. So they
devised a plan to have Jesus arrested. How to pull it off was the
problem. Some Pharisee lawyer probably devised this apparently foolproof plan.

Part of the plan may even have involved entrapping this
woman. Let's face it, it's very unlikely they would have actually
caught two people in the act of sexual sin. If they did, the law
clearly taught that both should be put to death. But notice we
don't read about the guilty *man* in this story. We just read about
the woman. That raises the possibility that she was entrapped.
If she was, that fact would not relieve her of responsibility. But
clearly, this whole thing sounds like a setup designed to put
Jesus in a quandary.

The Pharisees thought that Jesus would not know how to handle this problem because it was a bit of a dilemma. If Jesus had said to stone the woman, then the people might have withdrawn from Him. On the other hand, if Jesus had said to let her go, He would be defying the law and, in effect, telling people to disregard it and live as they pleased.

Some people interpret loving patience and a willingness to forgive as leniency, thinking God is something of a soft touch—a pushover. But the Bible clearly says that "through the Lord's mercies we are not consumed" (Lamentations 3:22). Don't confuse mercy with leniency.

Some people commit sin and think they are getting away with it. At the same time, there are some who, in their own warped minds, think that the Lord is actually telling them what they are doing is okay!

I knew a lonely man who was praying that he would find a wife. Before long, he met a nice young woman. There was just one problem—she was already married!

"I'm really asking the Lord what I should do," he said to me.

I told him that he no longer needed to pray for direction concerning this situation, because God had plainly addressed it in His Word. The Scripture tells us not to commit adultery. If a woman is married and you involve yourself with her, that is adultery.

"But we're in love," he protested. "We feel so good about this."

It doesn't matter. God says no. That's it. It's simple.

As you live a little longer, you start seeing how much sense God's commandments actually make. You realize He is not out there to spoil our fun. Nor is He trying to ruin our lives. He is trying to place barriers of protection—guardrails—in our lives to keep us from destroying ourselves, from falling off the cliff. But, sadly, our society has largely disregarded His laws. And we are reaping the inevitable, tragic results.

The purpose of the devious plan hatched by the Pharisees was to trap Jesus or to discredit Him. But Jesus turned the tables on them. Instead of passing judgment on the woman, He passed judgment on the judges. He was outraged that they would be so quick to condemn another person but not judge themselves. He decided to give them a little assistance and identify a sin for them to judge in their own lives.

Jesus stooped down and wrote on the ground. That's interesting. Why? Because this is the only record in the Bible of Jesus actually writing something. However, it is not the only time God wrote. We know the Ten Commandments were written with the finger of God. His personal autograph was on those two tablets that He gave to Moses on Mount Sinai. We also know that the hand of God wrote a message of judgment on the wall for wicked King Belshazzar, who had gone out of his way to mock and defy God at a great feast by praising false gods and drinking wine from the gold cups stolen from the temple.

But this is the only time during Jesus' earthly ministry that we know He wrote something. Here was the great lawgiver, Jesus Himself, turning the white light of the law on those who were so quick to quote it. Basically He said, "All right, boys, you like to quote the law to condemn others. Let's see how you fare under its searching light." And Jesus wrote.

What did He write? Judging from the response, it had to be significant. What happened? Everyone cleared out, from the oldest to the youngest. I can assure you He wasn't doodling. He wasn't saying, "Ticktacktoe anyone?" What did He write? We wonder. Some of the greatest minds in the church have grappled with this question for hundreds of years. I don't pretend to know what He wrote, but I will give you some possibilities:

Perhaps He wrote the Ten Commandments. Maybe He underlined certain commandments and then looked up at various individuals, locking His holy eyes with theirs with a look implying, "I know you are breaking this commandment."

Maybe He reminded them of the statement He had made in the Sermon on the Mount: "You have heard that it was said to those of old, 'You shall not commit adultery.' But I say to you that whoever looks at a woman to lust for her has already committed adultery with her in his heart" (Matthew 5:27-28). He could have implied that even though these self-righteous judges had not committed the act itself, to want in their hearts to do it was still sin before God.

Perhaps he wrote the secrets of their lives. Many people have a secret sin they hope will never be uncovered. Some people in the church today live double lives, appearing to be something they really aren't. But they are not fooling Jesus. Psalm 44:20 says, "If we had forgotten the name of our God or spread out our hands to a foreign god, would not God have discovered it, since he knows the secrets of the heart?" (NIV). We are also told in Romans 2:16 that our sins will be uncovered "in the day when God will judge the secrets of men by Jesus Christ." There are no secrets with God. Secret sin on earth is open scandal in heaven. God sees all. There is nothing that escapes His attention.

Jesus might have looked at one of those men and written what that particular individual was involved in. Can you imagine? I can just see that man looking into the eyes of God in human form and saying, "I really have to be going."

When they had all left, Jesus said, "Woman, where are those accusers of yours?" (John 8:10). It is fascinating that He refers to her as "Woman." This is a term of endearment in that culture—a word spoken with great tenderness and even respect. It would be like calling someone a lady in our culture. This woman wasn't used to being treated with such kindness and respect. Maybe she was a prostitute. Maybe she had always been looked down upon, like that friendless Samaritan woman Jesus encountered at the well who also lived immorally.

God Sees What You Can Become

God doesn't look at us the way this world does. We look in the mirror and see our flaws. God looks at us and sees what He can make of us. We see our shortcomings and mistakes. But God sees us and says, "I see what you can be."

God sees potential in us. He sees what He can make us into. Everyone else in this story saw a pitiful wench who lived an immoral lifestyle. Jesus saw a lady. "Woman, where are your accusers?" he asked. Then He added, "Neither do I condemn you" (John 8:11).

How His words must have shocked this undoubtedly hardened woman! She had possibly been used and abused by men all her life. Now the very men who had helped to destroy her were demanding her execution. But Jesus said, "Neither do I condemn you."

I wonder if she had even looked into His eyes up to that point. I envision this whole scene as one where she was mercilessly thrown in a heap at the feet of Jesus. Resigned to her fate, she probably thought to herself, *I knew this day would eventually come. Time has run out for me. I've been set up once again, but this time I'll pay with my life. This pretty much sums up my whole miserable existence on this earth. But what does it matter?*

All of a sudden, to her surprise, her accusers are summarily dismissed by this mysterious man called Jesus. Perhaps for the first time that day she lifted up her eyes and gazed deeply into His. And there she saw the very eyes of God. Instead of seeing scorn and hatred, she saw eyes that burned with a deep love and tender compassion.

How can Jesus say that He didn't condemn her? Because a short time after this He was going to the cross, and He knew it.

All of the sin of the world was going to be poured upon Him. Every sin this woman had ever committed was going to be put on Him—the Son of God. He was saying, "I will not condemn you, because I am going to face the condemnation that you should face. I am going to pay the price for your sin. Neither do I condemn you."

Notice, too, that He didn't say, "Go and sin no more, and as a result I will not condemn you." He didn't say, "Live a perfect and flawless life, and then maybe I will find it in My heart to forgive you." If that were the case, who could make it? Rather, He said, "Neither do I condemn you." Now, as a result of that recognition, "Go and sin no more." In other words, He said, "I accept you. I love you. I forgive you. Now, go and sin no more."

We don't live godly lives to win or find God's approval. God already loves us. God will accept us no matter what we have done. He will throw His arms around us and receive us. But then He wants to change us.

A Challenge to Change

Jesus' act of forgiveness of this woman was followed by a challenge. He didn't forgive her and say, "Go out. Party. Have fun. Live as you please." He said, "There needs to be a change in your life. Don't keep living this way. I have a new way of living for you—a life with the greatest freedom available but one that has clear parameters for your own protection."

Was this leniency? Not at all. Jesus was going to die for her sin in a short time. Forgiveness may be free, but it certainly isn't cheap. And God offers that forgiveness to us.

We may say, "What do I have to do to get it? Do I have to go through some ritual? What can I do to earn forgiveness?"

"Absolutely nothing," God says.

Well, it must not be worth much, some might think. Not true! There's no way we could ever pay the price—no matter how much money we had, no matter how much time we had. We could never afford or deserve the gift of God. It cost Jesus His very life.

But we are suspicious of anything free, aren't we? When someone says, "We have a free offer for you," we wonder, *What's the catch?*

I remember some years ago I was given free tickets to Disneyland. I went with my family. One of the people who was going to join us didn't show up. So I had the extra ticket in my back pocket. We went into the park and on some of the rides. Then I said to my wife, "You know, I have this extra ticket. I feel like someone should be using it. It's just going to waste if I keep it. And, who knows, there might be some person out there who doesn't have enough money to get in. So I'll just go out and give it to someone quickly. I'm sure it won't be hard getting rid of a ticket to Disneyland. I'll be back in just a few minutes."

I went outside and saw people waiting to get into the park. I went up to them and said, "Hi. I have this extra ticket to get you into the park. It's free. You want it? Here, it's yours."

"What do you want for it?" asked one guy.

"Nothing. It was given to me, and I didn't want to see it go to waste. Here, take it!"

"No, I don't want it," he said. He would rather pay for a ticket than take one from a stranger.

I went over to some other folks. The same scene repeated itself. Everyone I approached was apprehensive, suspicious. I found myself almost pleading. "Would you please take it?" Finally one person took it—grudgingly I might add.

Likewise, when we say God stands ready to pardon and forgive us, and it's free, there's some suspicion on our part. It just doesn't compute in our minds to think that God can forgive us without our doing anything to merit it.

Then He says, "Now, because of what I've done for you,

I want you to make those appropriate changes in your lifestyle." It's the goodness of God that leads me to repentance, the Bible says. But what about the woman? Did she become a believer? Did she turn to Jesus in faith? I suggest she did. It's indicated in her answer to His question, "Where are your accusers?"

She said, "I don't have any, Lord." She called Him "Lord." This woman believed right there. She said, "That's it. I need no additional convincing. I believe."

Did you know that life-changing belief can take place that quickly? Sometimes we hear people say, "I'm in the process of converting to Christianity." But, in truth, we're either converted, or we're not. We may go through a process of checking out the claims of Christ. We may go through a process of learning more about what it is to be a Christian. But the actual moment of conversion is immediate. It doesn't take years. It doesn't take months. It doesn't take days. It doesn't even take hours. It happens instantaneously, as it happened to this woman. Suddenly it just all comes into focus for us, and we say, "Lord, I believe. I have seen enough." We change our minds, our hearts, and our direction—we are converted.

That's what Jesus did for the woman in this story. There are three promises He made to her:

1. *Her sins could be forgotten.* He didn't mention her past. He didn't say, "Now let's talk about all those things you have done wrong in your life. We should examine each one carefully." Instead He said, "Neither do I condemn you." Jesus completely forgave her past sins.

The same thing happens to us when we put our faith in Christ. As I mentioned in an earlier chapter, that is part of the salvation process known as "justification." Scripture tells us, "Brothers! Listen! In this man Jesus there is forgiveness for your sins! Everyone who trusts in him is freed from all guilt and declared righteous [justified]—something the Jewish law could never do" (Acts 13:38-39, TLB).

Maybe you've continued to be plagued by what you did before you came to Christ. You are riddled with guilt, and as a result, you don't feel as if you are moving forward in your walk with God. Remember, God has not only forgiven but forgotten your sins: "I will forgive their wickedness and will remember their sins no more" (Jeremiah 31:34, NIV).

Certainly the devil is not happy with this. He loves to dredge up failures from our past. He loves to hit that play button in the video player of our imagination. Then rewind, play, rewind, play, over and over until we sink into despair. But God says, "I have forgotten those sins!" God does not wish us to remember what he is willing to forget.

In Micah 7 we read, "Who is a God like you, who pardons sin and forgives the transgression of the remnant of his inheritance? You do not stay angry forever but delight to show mercy. You will again have compassion on us; you will tread our sins underfoot and hurl all our iniquities into the depths of the sea" (vv. 18-19, NIV). Think about it! God has released you from the guilt and penalty of all the sins you have ever committed. He has taken them and thrown them into the sea of forgetfulness, and He's posted a sign that reads No Fishing Allowed!

Justification speaks not only of what God has taken away (our sin) but also of what He has put in its place. When God justifies people, He does so by placing to our credit all of the righteousness of Christ. This balances the moral and spiritual budget for us.

This is not a gradual process. It's immediate. Instantaneous. Yet many Christians fail to even glance at what God has placed in their spiritual bank accounts. They live as spiritual paupers instead of children of the King.

A homeless man once stopped a well-dressed and

successful lawyer on the street and asked him for a dollar. Taking a long, hard look at this man's face, the attorney said, "Don't I know you from somewhere?"

"You should," said the homeless man. "I'm your former classmate. Remember, English, third period?"

"Why, Steve, of course, I know you!" the lawyer answered. Without further question, the lawyer wrote a check for five hundred dollars to his old classmate. "Here, take this and get a new start. I don't care what's happened in the past—it's the future that counts!"

Tears welled up in the man's eyes as he walked to a bank nearby. Stopping at the door, he looked through the glass and saw the well-dressed tellers and the spotlessly clean interior. Then he looked at the filthy rags he was wearing and said to himself, *They won't take this from me. They'll swear that I forged it.*

The next day the two men met again. The lawyer noticed there had been no change in Steve's appearance. "Why, Steve!" exclaimed the attorney. "What did you do with my check? Gamble it away? Drink it up?"

The homeless man said, "No," as he pulled it out of his dirty shirt pocket and told why he hadn't cashed it.

"Listen, friend," said the lawyer, "what makes that check good is not your clothes or appearance but my signature. Go on, cash it!"

And this time the man did.

Just as Jesus justified the woman caught in adultery, he has justified us. We no longer have to be plagued by guilt and shame. We have a new beginning and a fresh start in life.

2. *She did not need to fear Judgment Day.* In a relatively short period of time, Jesus Himself would face the judgment she deserved for all the sins she had committed in life. The Lord didn't condemn her, nor does He condemn us. The Bible says, "There is therefore now no condemnation to those who are in

Christ Jesus" (Romans 8:1). She didn't have to be afraid of Judgment Day, which also meant she didn't have to be afraid of death.

3. *He gave her new power to face her problems.* Jesus told her, "Go and sin no more." Once you become a Christian, God gives you the strength to live the way He wants you to live.

We sometimes look at our lives and say, "I can't do that. There's no way I will ever change. I can't be a Christian. It's too hard. It's unobtainable." That's looking at it backward. It's not us doing it for God. It will be God doing it through us. Yes, He wants our cooperation. Yes, He wants us to yield. But He will give us the strength to do what He wants us to do. Being a Christian is inviting Jesus Christ to live inside of us—not just believing in a historical Jesus, not just trying to emulate His example or model. It is Christ Himself coming into our lives and changing us.

Have you been caught in the act of your own sin? Have you been playing around with it? The same Jesus who gave the adulterous woman a new lease on life so many years ago is ready to pardon you right now. And guess what? He knows you. You may not know Him yet, but He knows you. He knows all about your life. He knows all about your thoughts. He knows what you are planning right now. He knows what you are up to. He knows what you are trying to hide. Remember, there are no secrets with God.

At the same time, He loves you unconditionally. He wants to pardon you. He wants to say to you, "Go and sin no more. Don't live this way anymore. I will give you the strength to do it." But you must come to Him and ask for His forgiveness—ask Him for a second chance.

A SECOND CHANCE FOR
THE HARDENED HEART

*For you were like sheep going astray, but have now returned
to the Shepherd and Overseer of your souls.*
  1 PETER 2:25

Steven Funk remembers looking around his Vietnamese village
in 1982 and dreaming of a better life. A sister and brother had
already made the long pilgrimage to the United States and now
lived in the promised land of California. But twelve-year-old
Stevie, as he was called, wondered how such dreams could
ever come true.

One day his father asked Stevie to accompany him on a
one-week journey to a distant fishing village. Stevie packed
enough food and provisions for seven days, said good-bye to
his mother, and off they went. Along the way Stevie noticed
that his father was picking up other people as they made their
way to their destination. By the time they reached the sea, he
learned that he and his father were actually escaping to the
West. They would never return home again.

It was exciting at first, Stevie recalls. A total of fifteen
people—all adults except for him—piled into a small boat for
what was supposed to be a one-week sail to Singapore. But
soon after they embarked on their trip, a big storm ravaged the
boat, leaving it floating aimlessly at sea. They drifted and drifted
until they ran out of food and water. It got so bad that one man,

delirious from thirst, drank gasoline and died a horrible and slow death before the eyes of the other passengers.

"At that time, I didn't really care," remembers Stevie. "All I thought about was my own survival."

A few days later there was still no help in sight. Other passengers, including Stevie's father, began to fade from starvation and dehydration. Several more died.

"I was getting weaker and weaker," remembers Stevie. "I looked up into the sky and asked God to let me live. In Vietnam I had been a bad boy. I used to steal things and rob people and beat them up. But I asked God for forgiveness. I said, 'If there is a God out there, please save me from this journey. I'm a sinner and a bad boy. If You save me from this journey, I will tell all my friends.' I didn't know Jesus then, but I prayed to God from my heart."

The next day it rained, providing Stevie and the other surviving passengers with water to sustain them. Soon they spotted an island. But by the time they managed to paddle to it, five of the fifteen people aboard had died, and Stevie's father was very weak. Unfortunately, there was little on the island to give them much encouragement—no trees, no animals, no fruit, only bird eggs, which they ate raw.

The eggs were not enough to revive some of the weakest people. One day Stevie's father told him, "I'm not going to make it, but if you do, just try to be the best you can." To this day— fourteen years later—recalling this moment still chokes Stevie up. His father died shortly thereafter.

The stranded shipmates became increasingly desperate for survival. One day a man came up to Stevie and offered him meat. Stevie thought about it and wondered where it came from, but survival and hunger were his overriding concerns. He ate, knowing the meat was probably human flesh but not caring too much.

"I don't really feel proud that I ate those people," said

Stevie of the other passengers who died of starvation and exposure. "But you do it to survive."

Although the island was deserted and often reached the stifling temperature of 120 degrees, there was one thing the castaways found useful—a lighthouse. They managed to knock out the beacon, hoping its absence would serve to attract attention to their plight. Finally, when there were only six people still alive, a ship came to see why the beacon was out. It had been twenty-seven days since the boat left Vietnam for what was supposed to be a seven-day excursion. But the horrors were not over yet.

According to Stevie, the Chinese sailors on the rescue ship were superstitious. They believed it was bad luck to take aboard a passenger who was paralyzed, as was one of the survivors. No amount of pleading would change their minds. So a fully conscious man, the brother of another survivor, was tossed unceremoniously overboard to a waiting school of sharks.

The ship took the survivors to Hong Kong. All of their hair had fallen out due to starvation. In fact, Stevie was the only survivor who did not have some permanent disability from the ordeal. One had gone insane, one had lost the use of a leg, another had hearing loss. Stevie had lost touch with his entire family.

Miraculously, a few days after he got to Hong Kong, a stranger asked him about his family and name. The man claimed to know Stevie's mother and his sister's address in the United States. Apparently, after her husband and son had left, Stevie's mother sent telegrams to her children in California alerting them to the plan. The sister, in turn, understanding the risks and hazards of the sea, contacted the boat-people organizations in Singapore, Thailand, and Hong Kong with information about her little brother and father. Two weeks later, his sister wired the funds for Stevie to come to California.

"When I got to the U.S., it was so different from what I had known," recalls Steve Funk, now an auto body mechanic in Stanton, California. "There was everything I could ever want—cars, schools, nice homes. I had everything, but I wasn't happy, because I had forgotten about God and the promise I had made to Him. I partied, took drugs, and did every bad thing I could think of. My life was empty."

It so happened that someone invited Steve to one of our evangelistic crusades. I preached about Jonah, another man on a boat who tried to run from God. I told how God gave Jonah a second chance, and He would do the same for us if we would admit our sins and turn to Him by faith. Steve heard God speak to him that night, and he responded with thousands of others.

"I felt right away that something was right about this," he remembered. In 1995, Steve Funk became a Christian. He credits God with saving him from that disastrous journey fourteen years earlier and with saving his spiritual life later in America.

"I got a second chance," Steve said. "In fact, I even got a third chance."

Dealing with a Spiritual Stiff Neck

Like so many of us, Steve Funk tried to run from God—to run from a solemn commitment that he had made, a commitment he credits with saving his life. Maybe you can identify with Steve. In a moment of crisis we call out to God and make promises to Him. But then, as time goes by and life returns to normal, those promises fall by the wayside. We know we should make good on them sometime, but we want to decide when.

In truth, when we keep delaying coming back to God, we are actually resisting the Holy Spirit. In the book of Acts, when Stephen stood before the Sanhedrin prior to his execution, he took advantage of the moment and gave a compelling presentation of the gospel. He obviously didn't take the timid approach with these unbelieving members of the Sanhedrin. He pinpointed their problem with accepting his message by saying, "You stiff-necked people, with uncircumcised hearts and ears! You are just like your fathers: You always resist the Holy Spirit!" (Acts 7:51, NIV).

What did he mean by that? According to Scripture, one aspect of the Holy Spirit's work in the world is to bring the unbeliever into a relationship with God (see John 16:13). He wants to help us see our need for the Savior. He is very patient and incredibly persistent. But it is possible to resist His pleading. As God Himself says in Genesis 6:3, "My Spirit will not contend with man forever" (NIV). It appears that these spiritual leaders of Israel had been convinced of the truth of what Stephen was telling them, but they simply would not yield their hearts.

Likewise, we resist the Holy Spirit when we say, "I know that the message of the gospel is true. I know that Jesus Christ is the One I should follow. But I don't want to become a Christian. I don't want to change my lifestyle. I don't want to change the way I am. I don't want to live differently than I am living now."

We were created to yield ourselves to God. We were created ultimately to join God in heaven. We may have lost our way, but we must not lose our destination's address. We can't deny the hunger that is in our souls. We shouldn't say, "Earth satisfies us, and everything we want and long for we have found in this life." We know that's not true. We know there's something in us that drives us on. We're not going to find happiness and satisfaction in this life completely. There will be those moments, yes. There will be those times when it seems perfect. But then reality sets in. It's a homesickness for heaven. God has put this homing instinct in us, and it will only be satisfied when we yield ourselves to Him and see Him face-to-face.

Have you ever wondered if God would forgive you or if He would extend to you a second chance as He did to Steve Funk? Have you ever worried that perhaps you have gone too far—

beyond the point of no return? Is it possible to go too far—to push God to the point where He will not forgive us any longer? Is there such a thing as an unpardonable sin? If so, what is it?

Let's consider the story of the Prodigal Son again. Imagine what might have happened if, after a few months of being home, the Prodigal Son got tired of hanging around with good old Dad. What would have happened if he had said, "Dad, I'm leaving again. I'm returning to my old prodigal life." Let's say he went out and committed the same sins again and once again returned home repentant. Would the father have forgiven him a second time? Yes! Suppose he did it a third time. Would the prodigal have been forgiven a third time? Yes, he would have. A fourth time? A fifteenth time? Would he have been forgiven? Again and again the answer is yes.

Similarly, if we sin against God, will He forgive us? Absolutely. If we have blown it more than once, will He still forgive us? Yes. He will forgive us again and again and again. No matter what we have done, what sins we have committed, God stands ready to forgive us if we will come to Him truly repentant. He will forgive us for embezzling money, for cheating on our spouses, and, yes, even for committing murder!

The question is not whether God will forgive us but whether we truly and sincerely want to be forgiven. The Bible warns us that continuing in sin leads to a hardened heart.

"He who is often rebuked, and hardens his neck, will suddenly be destroyed, and that without remedy," says Proverbs 29:1. Then we are told in Hebrews 3:12-13, "See to it, brothers, that none of you has a sinful, unbelieving heart that turns away from the living God. But encourage one another daily, as long as it is called Today, so that none of you may be hardened by sin's deceitfulness" (NIV).

Make no mistake about it: Sin is powerful. It is illusive. It is tricky. It can appear so appealing on the outside. I have seen people who know better, people who have walked with the Lord for years and know His Word well, fall into sin and be deceived by it. We all must be very careful.

The great evangelist Billy Sunday said that the problem with a lot of people is that they treat sin like a cream puff instead of the rattlesnake that it is. Speaking of a rattlesnake, have you ever seen a baby one? Compared with an adult, it is actually kind of cute. It looks like a miniature rattlesnake with a small body, tiny rattle, and little fangs. When you see one, the temptation is to say, "Look at that little baby rattler. He's so little, what possible harm could he do? I think I'll pick him up." But people familiar with snakes and snakebites will tell you there is no more danger-ous rattler than the baby. Although they are smaller, their bites tend to be more venomous. Why? Some think it is because the babies, in their excited and nervous state, tend to release more venom in their attacks than the more mature snakes.

Don't be fooled by what appear to be small misdeeds. Not only good things come in small packages. Sometimes dynamite comes in small packages. Sometimes poison. What happens when we yield to smaller temptations and lesser sins is that it conditions us for bigger ones.

Woody Allen made an interesting movie several years ago called *Crimes and Misdemeanors*. Unlike most of his films, this was not a comedy. It was a serious drama about a successful doctor who had an extramarital affair. After a while his mistress was no longer willing to play second fiddle to the doctor's wife. But the man had no intention of divorcing his wife. The mistress threatened to tell his wife everything and ruin his marriage unless he moved toward divorce. Ultimately, this law-abiding, upstanding citizen decided that the only way out was to have his mistress murdered. The point of the story was that one seemingly small indiscretion can lead to much more serious offenses.

This is not to say that adultery is a minor infraction. Note that it made God's top-ten list of things we should not do (the Ten Commandments), suggesting to me that it's a serious sin, indeed. However, the world has a much different way of looking at it. Adultery is not a crime anymore in our enlightened society. Murder, however, is still frowned upon in most cases.

True believers will always come back to God after going astray, as the Prodigal Son did. We will never be happy doing the old things again. We will never find satisfaction and contentment in the things of the world. Before we were Christians, we didn't know any better. Our worldview was that life was basically meaningless and that we should get all we could out of it while we could. In other words, "Eat, drink, and be merry, for tomorrow we die." Then one day when we committed our lives to Christ, we recognized that there is indeed a God. Not only that, but we also recognized that there is a devil, heaven, hell, right, wrong—there is a purpose to life. Now we know better. If we try to go back to those old things, they will never fill the void in our lives. They will only harden our hearts.

The Prodigal Pig?

We've heard all about the Prodigal Son, but have you heard the story of the prodigal pig? That's in the Bible, too. It's mentioned in 2 Peter 2:21-22: "For it would have been better for them not to have known the way of righteousness, than having known it, to turn from the holy commandment delivered to them. But it has happened to them according to the true proverb: 'A dog returns to his own vomit,' and, 'a sow, having washed, to her wallowing in the mire.' "

I have personally witnessed the truth of this proverb. I have watched my dog return to his own vomit. I have also noticed lately that pigs are becoming more popular as pets. Pigs are supposed to be very intelligent animals. The hit movie *Babe* made pigs even more popular. A friend of mine purchased a Vietnamese pot-bellied pig as a pet some time ago. He took the pig along with his family everywhere—even to the beach.

"They get sunburned, though, you know," my friend said, "so we have to put sunscreen on him."

"You actually take a pig to the beach and put sunscreen on him?" I asked.

"Of course."

"Don't forget the sunglasses," I suggested.

The point of this proverb is that you can take a pig, shower him, put some nice cologne on him, and even dress him up in a little custom-made piggy tuxedo if you want. Or you can slather him with sunscreen and get him his own little piggy beach chair to sit in while wearing his specially designed piggy sunglasses.

But let me tell you something: The first chance that pig gets, he's going to make a beeline back to the slop. Why? Because that's where he wants to be. It's a pig. Pigs are meant to act like pigs. It's their nature.

A prodigal will always return home because a prodigal is a child of God who has gone astray. But a pig will always go back to the mud. The question we must ask ourselves is, "Are we pigs, or are we prodigals?" I know that sounds strange. Let me say it another way: Are we really children of God, or are we just pretending to be?

The Bible asks an important question that we all should consider: "Check up on yourselves. Are you really Christians? Do you pass the test? . . . Or are you just pretending to be Christians when actually you aren't at all?" (2 Corinthians 13:5, TLB).

The Bible says in 1 John 2:19, "They went out from us, but they did not really belong to us. For if they had belonged to us, they would have remained with us; but their going showed that none of them belonged to us" (NIV).

We all know people who have fallen away spiritually.

Sometimes people make changes in their lives, go to church, get all excited about the Bible, and then they suddenly turn their backs on it all. Usually we say, "Oh, isn't it sad they have backslidden." But I suggest to you that many of these people never were true believers to begin with. The real test is where they end up, because a true believer will always come back home eventually. A person who is not a true believer won't.

Are you a prodigal or a pig? Are you a believer or an unbeliever? Are you a child of God or a child of the devil? It might sound harsh, but those are really the only choices we have in life. First John 3:9-10 says, "No one who is born of God will continue to sin, because God's seed remains in him; he cannot go on sinning, because he has been born of God. This is how we know who the children of God are and who the children of the devil are: Anyone who does not do what is right is not a child of God" (NIV).

That verse is not saying that if you are a Christian you will never sin. All Christians sin. In fact, the Bible says, "If we say that we have no sin, we deceive ourselves, and the truth is not in us" (1 John 1:8). Every one of us is going to fail. We are going to fall at times. But there is a difference between the person who sins and is repentant and the person who lives in a constant lifestyle of sin. There is a difference between the person who stumbles and wants to get up again and the person who couldn't care less. If you are a prodigal, you will always come home. If you are a pig, you will return to the mire.

Children of God return home because of a prompting within their conscience called the conviction of the Holy Spirit. Everyone—believer and unbeliever alike—has a conscience, but the Holy Spirit works like a warning system within the conscience of believers, giving them a better sense of right and wrong and reminding them of the absolute standards found in Scripture. Those who are not true believers won't sense that conviction at all. They will go out and do whatever they want to do. Their hearts will be so hard they won't care about right or wrong. On the other hand, some people don't want to hear about God. They say, "I have heard all this stuff before. I tried the whole Christianity thing. I went to church and all that. I tried it, but it didn't work for me." To those people I would suggest that the problem is not with God, it's with them.

Anyone who says that Christianity didn't work for them has either never met Christ personally or didn't do what Christ says to do. Jesus works for everyone. He's not some kind of product that doesn't work for everyone and can be discarded if they're unsatisfied.

He is God Almighty, and His promises are true for every person who responds appropriately to them. There are no exceptions.

When I heard the gospel before I was a Christian, I would think, *I can't do that. I'm not the religious type. I wasn't raised in church. I'm not Mr. Goody Two-Shoes*. I didn't think I would fit in with Christians and the church. I didn't think it would work for me. But I was wrong, because I was not dealing with an "it," but rather a "Him." God can and will change all sincere people who put their faith in Him as Savior and Lord of their lives.

Perhaps you've been trying to run from God. God wants to forgive you, no matter what you have done. That's right, no matter what. Can you go too far? Yes. There is a point of no return. Does that mean there is a point at which God would not forgive you? The Bible does talk about an "unforgivable sin." But the question you should probably really concern yourself with is this: Is there a point at which, because of your hardened heart, you would not want to be forgiven?

Jesus warns about the unforgivable sin. It is called the blasphemy of the Holy Spirit. What does that mean? The work of the Holy Spirit, who is God, is to show us our need for Jesus Christ.

He comes into the world to convict us of our sin, to bring us to our senses. To blaspheme Him means to insult Him, to resist Him, to turn away from Him. The ultimate insult is when we have so sealed ourselves off that we don't even sense His touch any longer. We have gone too far. How tragic that would be.

Many people will harden their hearts to the truth of God's Word. How do we get hardened hearts? By continued exposure to the truth of God and refusal to obey and respond to it. We know it's true. We accept it intellectually. But we don't personally respond. And when we do this, we become hardened by the very truth that should have softened us. It just goes to show that contact with holy things, if it does not convert, actually hardens the heart. It shows that the light of Jesus Christ, if it does not convert listeners, plunges them into deeper darkness. "The same sun that softens the wax, hardens the clay." We become "educated unbelievers." That is why the most difficult people to reach with the gospel are those who know it best.

After I preached one night on this very subject, two young men came to speak to me. One was obviously very upset and had an extremely distressed look on his face. As he told me what was troubling him, it all began to make sense.

This young man was convinced that he had blasphemed the Holy Spirit. He thought there was no forgiveness for him, ever. No wonder he looked distressed!

I asked him if he believed that Jesus Christ was the Son of God.

He said, "Yes."

I then asked if he had repented of his sin and asked Jesus to come into his heart and life.

Again, he said, "Yes."

As I inquired more into why he thought he had committed this unpardonable sin, he told me that he thought that somewhere in his unbelieving days when he had cursed God, he was sure he had cursed the Holy Spirit as well.

What a privilege it was to reassure him that his actions were not what Jesus was referring to and to tell him that God had indeed forgiven him. His friend later wrote me a letter and told me of the radical transformation in this man's life upon hearing of God's gracious forgiveness.

It's interesting to note that the apostle Paul, once he received the forgiveness of Christ, never dwelled upon his past. He moved forward. If he were around today, I'm sure that some well-meaning people might suggest that he go into counseling for his violent past of hunting down the early believers. He could have been paralyzed by guilt, rendering him ineffective. Instead, Paul dedicated himself to one thing and one thing alone: "Forgetting what is behind and straining toward what is ahead, I press on toward the goal to win the prize for which God has called me heavenward in Christ Jesus" (Philippians 3:13-14, NIV).

People who have committed the unpardonable or unfor-givable sin would not be concerned, much less worried, about it. It would be the people who are so hard, so callous and indif-ferent, that they have hearts of stone. I'm sure this takes place over a period of time. Then again, every time the decision to receive Christ is put off, one would be a step closer. It's certainly not a sin a believer should ever worry about commit-ting. But it is one that unbelievers should seriously consider.

Everybody makes mistakes. The trick in life is simply not to make the biggest mistake of all—not allowing yourself to be forgiven. There's forgiveness for everyone—everyone, that is, who will accept it. Many people have committed serious sins in their lives but have found second chances. You can too. No matter what you have done or think you have done, there is still room for forgiveness, redemption, and second chances. Only one human being ever lived a perfect life on earth. And He's the reason we have second chances.

Don't let sin harden your heart and make you oblivious to what is taking place in your life. Get out of the rat race and into God's grace with your life.

A SECOND CHANCE TO FOLLOW GOD'S WILL

Those who cling to worthless idols forfeit the grace that could be theirs. But I, with a song of thanksgiving, will sacrifice to you. What I have vowed I will make good. Salvation comes from the Lord.
JONAH 2:8-9, NIV

A young girl was sharing her faith out on a street corner one day. An older man—an intellectual and well-known atheist—decided to have a little fun at her expense. He walked up to her with the intention of embarrassing her. As she spoke, a little crowd began to gather. Finally, the man spoke up, his voice booming above the girl's.

"Young lady, excuse me," he said. "I have a question for you."

"Yes sir, what is it?" she asked, turning to the man.

"You say that you believe in the Bible," he said. "Is that true?"

"Oh, yes sir, I believe in the Bible," she replied. "I believe it is the Word of God and every word of it is inspired."

"Oh, is that so?" he responded. "Then I suppose you believe in all the miracles of the Bible."

"Absolutely," she said, "I believe in every miracle in the Bible."

"Then you must believe in the story of Jonah and the whale—that a man was actually swallowed by a whale and lived to tell about it? Do you believe that?"

"Yes sir, I do."

"Is that so? Well, tell me then, how is it possible that a man could live inside a whale for three days and three nights?"

"I don't know, sir, but when I get to heaven I will ask Jonah."

"Well," the man said, "what if he's not in heaven? What if he's in hell?"

"Well," she said, "then you can ask him."

The story of Jonah and the whale is the one that most of us have heard since childhood. In fact, it's one of those stories that skeptics like to cite as proof that the Bible is not true or meant to be accepted literally. It would be impossible, they say, for a man to survive in the belly of a fish for three days and three nights.

But the story of Jonah is not primarily about a man swallowed live by a huge fish or a whale. It is the story of a second chance. It is the story of God's forgiveness. We see a man who saw the futility of running from God and was given another opportunity for service.

Now the word of the Lord came to Jonah the son of Amittai, saying, "Arise, go to Nineveh, that great city, and cry out against it; for their wickedness has come up before Me." But Jonah arose to flee to Tarshish from the presence of the Lord. He went down to Joppa, and found a ship going to Tarshish; so he paid the fare, and went down into it, to go with them to Tarshish from the presence of the Lord.

But the Lord sent out a great wind on the sea, and there was a mighty tempest on the sea, so that the ship was about to be broken up.

Then the mariners were afraid; and every man cried out to his god, and threw the cargo that was in the ship into the sea, to lighten the load. But Jonah had gone down into the lowest parts of the ship, had lain down, and was fast asleep.

So the captain came to him, and said to him, "What do you mean, sleeper? Arise, call on your God; perhaps your God will consider us, so that we may not perish."

And they said to one another, "Come, let us cast lots, that we may know for whose cause this trouble has come upon us." So they cast lots, and the lot fell on Jonah. Then they said to him, "Please tell us! For whose cause is this trouble upon us? What is your occupation? And where do you come from? What is your country? And of what people are you?"

So he said to them, "I am a Hebrew; and I fear the Lord, the God of heaven, who made the sea and the dry land."

Then the men were exceedingly afraid, and said to him, "Why have you done this?" For the men knew that he fled from the presence of the Lord, because he had told them. Then they said to him, "What shall we do to you that the sea may be calm for us?"—for the sea was growing more tempestuous.

And he said to them, "Pick me up and throw me into the sea; then the sea will become calm for you. For I know that this great tempest is because of me."

Nevertheless the men rowed hard to return to land, but they could not, for the sea continued to grow more tempestuous against them. Therefore they cried out to the Lord and said, "We pray, O Lord, please do not let us perish for this man's life, and do not charge us with inno-cent blood; for You, O Lord, have done as it pleased You." So they picked up Jonah and threw him into the sea, and the sea ceased from its raging. Then the men feared the Lord exceedingly, and offered a sacrifice to the Lord and took vows.

> Now the Lord had prepared a great fish to swallow
> Jonah. And Jonah was in the belly of the fish three days
> and three nights. (Jonah 1:1-17)

Like the girl in my story, I don't pretend to know how Jonah
survived in the belly of the fish. But I do accept it as true. It is a
miracle of the Bible. Notice that the Bible says that the Lord
prepared a great fish to swallow Jonah. We assume it was a
whale. Maybe it was. Then again it is entirely possible that God
created a unique fish just to swallow the reluctant prophet.

God, of course, can do anything. The Bible is replete with
many miracles He brought about. To select one or two in an
attempt to discredit all of them is absurd. For instance, I believe
the first verse of the Bible, Genesis 1:1: "In the beginning God
created the heavens and the earth." If you accept that, the rest
of the miracles of the Bible will come relatively easy for you.

I believe that Jonah was swallowed by a fish and lived to
tell about it. If I needed any validation, it was provided by Jesus
Himself in response to the Pharisees' demand for a miracle sign,
recorded for us in Matthew 12:39-41:

> An evil and adulterous generation seeks after a sign, and
> no sign will be given to it except the sign of the prophet
> Jonah. For as Jonah was three days and three nights in the
> belly of the great fish, so will the Son of Man be three days
> and three nights in the heart of the earth. The men of
> Nineveh will rise up in the judgment with this generation
> and condemn it, because they repented at the preaching of
> Jonah; and indeed a greater than Jonah is here.

Not only did Jesus validate the story of Jonah as a miracle, but
He used it to illustrate His own crucifixion and resurrection
from the dead. Notice that Jesus called him "the prophet Jonah."

What a prophet he was! The place from which he prophesied was the bottom of the sea. The pulpit from which he preached was in the stomach of a fish. But let's not get stuck on the fish story. The real story is that Jonah was given a mission by God. He had a job to do and said, "No thanks." It's also the story of God's long-suffering patience and His willingness to forgive those who would stop running from Him and run to Him.

We shouldn't be too hard on Jonah, though. It's easy to see his shortcomings. He should have done what God told him to do. But in reality all Christians have been given marching orders from the Lord Himself. He told us to go into all the world and preach the gospel to every living person. How many of us are actually doing that?

Ignoring the Call of God

As the story begins, we see God calling Jonah. He said, "Go and preach to the city of Nineveh." A more literal rendering of what God said is, "Get up and go." Jonah got up and went all right, in the opposite direction, trying to escape from God and his own conscience.

God said, "Arise, go to Nineveh, that great city, and cry out against it; for their wickedness has come up before Me" (Jonah 1:2). Another way to translate this statement would be: "Their wickedness has reached a high degree," or "the highest pitch." The wickedness of Nineveh was overflowing. It was full to the brim. It was like an overflowing septic tank, and it stunk to high heaven. The city was so filled with sin that it was just coming over the top, and God said, "That's it! It stops now."

It is helpful to know a little background about the city of Nineveh. It was the capital of Assyria and was well known for its cruelty. Graphic accounts of the cruel treatment of captives have been found in Assyrian records. The Ninevites were known for their savagery in plundering cities. They burned

117

children alive, and they tortured adults by tearing the skin from their bodies, leaving them to die in the scorching sun. Perhaps that's why God said, "That's it! Enough is enough!"

It was a situation similar to Genesis 6:5-7, when the wickedness of man had become so great that God essentially said, "That's it. My Spirit shall not strive with man forever." But we can understand Jonah's reluctance to go and preach in such a place. Jonah was a patriotic Israelite. He loved his people. The Ninevites were their mortal enemies. When God said, "Go and preach to the Ninevites," Jonah was dismayed. He thought, *God, I know You. You have this tendency to forgive people. My fear is that You will let them off the hook. I'm actually rather pleased to know that You are going to judge and destroy them. That's one less enemy we will have to fight!* In other words, Jonah didn't care about the Ninevites. He didn't care that Nineveh was a city of tens of thousands of people who were bound for hell. His procrastination and personal prejudice were stronger than any passion he had for the lost. In fact, judgment for Nineveh suited him just fine.

Have you ever felt that way about someone? Some of us may take perverse pleasure in knowing that people who really bother us may be going to hell. Certainly that is not the kind of attitude we should have as believers. The truth is, we all deserve to go to hell. We all deserve the judgment of God. Jesus didn't say to us as Christians, "Hate your enemies and hope judgment comes to them soon." He said, "You have heard that it was said, 'You shall love your neighbor and hate your enemy.' But I say to you, love your enemies, . . . and pray for those who . . . persecute you" (Matthew 5:43-44).

Sometimes we Christians retreat into our own little ivory towers. We isolate ourselves from people who do not believe the same way we do. We don't want any contact with them out of fear that we might be contaminated. Here's the problem with that kind of attitude: How are they going to be saved if they don't have contact with someone who can tell them about the love of God? I'm not suggesting that God is somehow dependent on us. He can do the job fine without us. At the same time, He wants to use us as His instruments.

Paul asked a rhetorical question in the book of Romans: "How, then, can they call on the one they have not believed in? And how can they believe in the one of whom they have not heard? And how can they hear without someone preaching to them?" (Romans 10:14, NIV).

Jonah, like many of us at one time or another, probably prayed that God would use his life. He probably promised to do whatever God asked him to do. But then when that moment of spiritual closeness passes, or that promise we made in the middle of a desperate time is forgotten, we go back to our natural pattern of living and put God on the back burner. We stop listening to what He is telling us to do with our lives.

Here Jonah was given the mission of preaching to his enemies. When he was told to get up and go, he got up and went—the wrong way. Instead of going five hundred miles northeast to Nineveh, Jonah attempted to go two thousand miles west to Tarshish. Jonah fled "from the presence of the Lord" (Jonah 1:3). That's really quite laughable when you get right down to it. For in reality, we cannot flee from God's presence, although many have tried.

Jonah was living in disobedience to God. He found a ship going to Tarshish and paid the fare. Then the Bible tells us, "But the Lord sent out a great wind on the sea, and there was a mighty tempest on the sea, so that the ship was about to be broken up" (Jonah 1:4). I love those first three words: "But the Lord . . ." It means that God will always have the last word. No matter what we do, those three words, "But the Lord," will catch up to us. He will always do what He wants to do. He will always do what's right.

Jonah was God's child. He was a believer, albeit a wayward one, a disobedient one, at this time. But he was a believer, nonetheless. What does the Bible say about the way God deals with His children? It says, "Whom the Lord loves He chastens" (Hebrews 12:6). Because God loves us, He will seek to get our attention when we are going the wrong way.

We all know what that's like. When we cross the line, when we are about to do something we know is wrong, there is that little voice inside of us, that sense of conviction from the Holy Spirit, saying, "Don't do that; it's not right."

Open Doors for Disobedience

Notice how relatively easy it was for Jonah, circumstantially at least, to do the wrong thing. Actually, Satan opened all the doors for Jonah's disobedience. This is why we must be careful about putting too much stock in circumstances as a major factor in determining the will of God for our lives. For the devil, too, can open doors. As Christians, we should seek to find our primary guidance from the Word of God. I don't need to ask God if something may be His will when He has clearly told us in the pages of Scripture it is not.

When the storm hit, everybody on board that rocking ship cried out to his god. This is so typical of people in crisis. We've all been there. It's the oldest story in the world. It has been said, "There are no atheists in foxholes." When the chips are down, when our lives are on the line, we cry out to God. Who else are we going to cry out to? Are we going to say, "Career, save me now"? Will we say, "American Express, help me now"? Are we likely to say, "Drugs, come to my aid now"? No. We cry out to God. On this little storm-tossed ship, everybody did the same thing.

Many gods were represented on board this ship, which caused a good deal of confusion among the sailors. They didn't know which one was the right god. Everyone cried out to his own deity. The captain said, "Is this everyone?"

"Well, there is that Jonah guy," someone may have suggested. "He's in the lower deck sleeping."

"Then wake him up."

So they rushed below and shook the sleeping prophet. "Wake up," they said to Jonah. "Cry out to your God. You might have the right one. Come on."

Jonah then revealed to these men that he was the one responsible for the storm that had come. He was a Hebrew, running from the one true God. These men were mystified. Why had he done this? Why would someone who had a God this powerful in his life want to run from Him and His will—a God who obviously was interested in the direction Jonah's life took?

Jonah recognized what was wrong. "Men," Jonah said, "this storm is from God because of me. The only way to stop it is to throw me overboard!"

"No, Jonah," they said. "We are going to save you."

But as Jonah said, the storm only got worse, and so over the side went the prophet, into the cold, dark, raging sea. And the Lord was ready. Awaiting Jonah's arrival was an extremely large sea creature. Whether it was a huge fish or a whale we don't know with any real certainty. We do know, however, that God had prepared this particular creature for this specific purpose.

An Incredible Fish Story

Corroborating evidence from nonbiblical sources shows us just how possible it was for Jonah to be swallowed by a whale. The *Encyclopedia Britannica* points out that the average sperm whale has a mouth twenty feet long, fifteen feet high, and nine feet wide. Is that big enough for a human to be swallowed whole? You bet. That mouth would be larger than most rooms in an average house. Furthermore, the physiological structure of the sperm whale, along with its habits, would allow for a man to be swallowed alive, survive two or three days inside, and be vomited up.

Sperm whales feed largely on squid, which are sometimes the size of a man or even larger. Whalers have sometimes found a whole giant squid in a dead whale's stomach. Another thing we know about the stomachs of whales is that it is very hot inside—between 105 and 108 degrees.

I read a modern-day Jonah story that happened back in 1891. In February of that year, the crew of the whaling ship *The Star of the East* spotted a large sperm whale in the vicinity of the Falkland Islands. Two boats were launched, and in a short time one of the harpooners was able to spear the whale but not before the second boat capsized. One man drowned, and another man, named James Bartley, was lost at sea and presumed dead.

The whale was killed and drawn to the side of the ship. As was the custom, they began to remove the blubber from the whale while still at sea. The next day the crew got out their crane and hoisted up the whale to the deck of the ship. When the stomach was opened, James Bartley was found alive—unconscious, but alive—much to the shock of all on board. They were able to revive him, and he lived to tell the story. There were some permanent reminders of his brief sojourn into the whale's stomach, however. All the hair on his body was gone, and his eyes were a light blue color. But he lived, just as Jonah did.

Let's look at what happened to Jonah in the whale or fish: "Then Jonah prayed to the Lord his God from the fish's belly. And he said, 'I cried out to the Lord because of my affliction, and He answered me. Out of the belly of Sheol I cried, and You heard my voice. For You cast me into the deep, into the heart of the seas, and the floods surrounded me; all Your billows and

Your waves passed over me. Then I said, "I have been cast out of Your sight" '" (Jonah 2:1-4).

Later, he says, "When my soul fainted within me, I remembered the Lord; and my prayer went up to You, into Your holy temple. Those who regard worthless idols forsake their own Mercy. But I will sacrifice to You with the voice of thanksgiving; I will pay what I have vowed. Salvation is of the Lord" (2:7-9).

The Surrender of a Stubborn Heart

When did Jonah pray? After three days and three nights. That is stubbornness! Think about it. He was wrapped in seaweed; he no doubt had fish smacking him in the face. The temperature was around 108 degrees. But for three days, Jonah would not give in.

He could have possibly said, "I'm not praying. God is not getting his way in my life, no matter what!" Or, perhaps he just thought, *I have blown it too badly. God surely wouldn't hear the prayer of a man stuck in the stomach of a whale, who ended up here because of his own disobedience. God wouldn't hear the prayer of a man like me who has sinned against Him.*

The devil, of course, is always there to exploit such situations. When we have sinned, when we have failed, the devil is there whispering in our ears, "Do you think God would hear you? Don't you even think of praying. Don't you dare set foot in the church. You're not worthy, you hypocrite." We have to learn to ignore him. The devil is a liar. In fact, the Bible reminds us that he is the father of all lies.

Yet, this story reminds us that we can call out to God anywhere and anytime. Daniel prayed in a lions' den. Paul and Silas prayed in prison. Joseph prayed in a pit. Elijah prayed in a cave. And Jonah prayed himself right out of the stomach of a whale.

What is the only thing that stops God from hearing our

prayers? Is it location? Is it distance? No, it's sin. Sometimes we think that if we are in a church sanctuary, God will be more likely to hear our prayers. Not necessarily. He is with us everywhere. He will listen anytime, unless we are in a state of unacknowledged, unconfessed sin. Isaiah 59:1-2 says, "Surely the arm of the Lord is not too short to save, nor his ear too dull to hear. But your iniquities have separated you from your God" (NIV). That is the only barrier. All we have to do to remove that barrier is turn to Him in repentance.

Finally Jonah comes to his senses and says to God, "I will pay what I have vowed" (Jonah 2:9). Jonah remembered from where he had fallen. The Bible tells us, "Remember therefore from where you have fallen" (Revelation 2:5). You may not be in a whale's belly, but sometime in life everyone finds himself in a difficult situation—usually one brought on by sin. There is still always hope.

Some people find themselves addicted to drugs or alcohol. Others find themselves pregnant out of wedlock. Maybe your marriage is falling apart. Perhaps you are HIV-positive or have full-blown AIDS. Maybe you are caught up in a gang lifestyle. You may be involved in situations where it seems there is no way out. It seems hopeless. Don't believe it. There is hope for you. God is there. And He is offering you a second chance, just as He did for Jonah.

After Jonah got back into a right relationship with God, we are told: "So the Lord spoke to the fish, and it vomited Jonah onto dry land" (2:10). Whenever I think about this verse, I imagine Ninevite people out sunbathing at the beach.

"Nice day today," says one.

"Looks like a good swell," says another.

"What's that coming in? Is that a ship?"

"It looks like a—a—a whale! It's actually coming right up to the shore. In fact it's coming right up on the beach!"

Suddenly this massive whale opens its mouth and makes a

huge retching sound. It begins to vomit, and amidst the pile of tangled seaweed and decomposed fish rolls out the one and only Jonah. He has no hair. His skin is bleached white. His eyes are light blue. He's probably wrapped in seaweed. And no doubt he stinks to high heaven. The prophet has arrived!

A Second Chance to Say Yes to God

In the first part of the third chapter of this story is a key verse. In fact, it is this verse that promoted the idea for this book. It says, "Now the word of the Lord came to Jonah the second time, saying, 'Arise, go to Nineveh, that great city, and preach to it the message that I tell you' " (3:1-2). A second time. Jonah, the reluctant prophet, was given a second chance for service. But God took him back to square one.

What was Jonah running from? Nineveh. Where did God require Jonah to go? Nineveh. It was Nineveh or bust. As Christians, each of us will face a Nineveh in life. There will come a moment in our lives when we read something in the Bible we don't personally like. Or perhaps God will direct us in a certain direction through prayer, and we will resist. When that happens, that's our Nineveh.

Jonah was reluctant to do what God had directed him to do. Do you know what his problem was? He was prejudiced. He was an Israelite called to preach to the Ninevites, avowed enemies of Israel. Are you prejudiced? Are there certain people you don't want to be around? Don't be surprised if God calls your hand on that.

Jonah's message to the Ninevites wasn't exactly good news. The Bible tells that "Jonah arose and went to Nineveh, according to the word of the Lord. Now Nineveh was an exceedingly great city, a three-day journey in extent. And Jonah began to enter the city on the first day's walk. Then he cried out and said, 'Yet forty days, and Nineveh shall be overthrown!' " (3:3-4). Jonah didn't soft-pedal it. He didn't sugarcoat it. He didn't hire a public-relations agency to help him package this message. In fact, at this point he didn't even tell them of the promise of forgiveness. He didn't mention what God would do if they repented. In effect, he said, "Hey, guys, you are going to be dead in forty days. Just thought I would tell you. Just doing my part."

And what was the effect of Jonah's message? "So the people of Nineveh believed God, proclaimed a fast, and put on sackcloth, from the greatest to the least of them" (3:5). Surprise! They turned to God.

I, too, have a simple message to give. I am nothing more than God's delivery boy. My responsibility is to deliver the simple message that He has given to me. First John 1:3-4 says, "We proclaim to you what we have seen and heard, so that you also may have fellowship with us. And our fellowship is with the Father and with his Son, Jesus Christ. We write this to make our joy complete" (NIV). What I have seen and heard I am declaring to you. I want you to know this God. I want you to experience this joy that He has offered.

I love Paul's words along these lines: "So everywhere we go, we tell everyone about Christ. We warn them and teach them with all the wisdom God has given us, for we want to present them to God, perfect [or mature] in their relationship to Christ. I work very hard at this, as I depend on Christ's mighty power that works within me" (Colossians 1:28-29, NLT).

I have been given my marching orders from our commander in chief, Jesus Christ, who said for us to go into all the world and preach the gospel to every living creature. And when we give that message out, we don't need to gloss it over. We don't have to add to it, nor do we need to subtract anything from it.

As the years have gone by, I have become more convinced of the power of the gospel message. The apostle Paul said, "For

I am not ashamed of the gospel of Christ, for it is the power of God to salvation for everyone who believes" (Romans 1:16). The word that he uses for *power* is a Greek word that could be translated "dynamic." Paul was saying there is a "dynamic power" in the simple message of the gospel. Don't be ashamed of it. Don't be afraid to proclaim it. Let people know. That's our responsibility.

Sometimes we don't share our faith readily because we fear certain situations and people. That's probably how Jonah felt. When he walked across Nineveh, it took him three days to get from one side to the other. He was probably overwhelmed by its sheer size. So he boiled down his message to this: "Forty days and Nineveh will be overthrown." It was a negative message. I think Jonah knew better because of a revealing statement he made when he prayed, "Ah, Lord, was not this what I said when I was still in my country? Therefore I fled previously to Tarshish; for I know that You are a gracious and merciful God, slow to anger and abundant in lovingkindness, One who relents from doing harm" (Jonah 4:2).

If Jonah indeed knew all of this, why didn't he tell it to the Ninevites? Because he didn't want them to repent and be spared by His gracious and merciful God. He wanted the Lord to destroy them. So he only gave them half the message, probably hoping they would not heed it and thus have to face the inevitable consequences.

In the same way, sometimes people only deliver half the gospel message. The Bible is described as the sword of the Spirit. But some use the sword of the Spirit to decapitate people rather than using it as a surgeon would to make an incision to extend life. Sometimes we will hear a presentation of the gospel that offers judgment without forgiveness. God is portrayed as an angry, vengeful, hostile supreme being who is out to destroy everyone. On the other hand, we hear people talk about God's love, mercy, and forgiveness, but they never tell us that we need to turn from our sin. Either message is incomplete.

Amazingly, the Ninevites, after hearing only half the gospel, turned to God en masse. The Scripture does not tell us that they simply believed in a god, or in some force, or in the spirit in the sky. No. They believed in God—the true God, the living God.

Jonah's message was not, "Believe in God—whatever you perceive him or her to be." Nor was his message, "Believe my message. But if you don't feel good about it, you can believe whatever you want as long as you are true to yourself." No. There is only one God. Every other one is an imitation. There is only one God who can save. There's only one God who can forgive. It's not true that all roads lead to heaven. There's only one road that leads there. Jesus said, "I am the way, the truth, and the life. No one comes to the Father except through Me" (John 14:6). That was a radical and exclusive claim.

All of the other religions of the world may have some facets of truth, but even if one of those prophets, gurus, teachers, or individuals who claim to be God had died on a cross, it wouldn't have made any difference. It wouldn't matter if Buddha had died on a cross. It wouldn't have mattered if L. Ron Hubbard, the founder of Scientology, had died on a cross. It wouldn't matter if Joseph Smith, the founder of Mormonism, had died on a cross. It wouldn't matter if Mary Baker Eddy, the founder of Christian Science, had died on a cross. Because they were just people—mere mortals—and they never rose from the dead.

What was unique about the death of Jesus was not that a man died on a cross, but that the man who died on the cross was God—the only one qualified to bridge the gap between a holy God and sinful humanity, the only one who can forgive, the only one who can save. That's the message we need to proclaim.

Where do you find yourself today? Are you in the belly of a

fish, so to speak, stubbornly refusing to follow what God has asked you to do? Are you missing the closeness of fellowship you once had with the Lord? Or do you find yourself trying to follow what God has asked you to do but with improper motives? Charles H. Spurgeon once said, "He who makes God's glory the one and only aim before which all other things bow themselves, is the man to bring honor to his Lord."[1]

God is ready to give you a second chance to follow His call for your life. True, years may have passed, and your circumstances may be different. Maybe you can't go to the foreign mission field you felt called to during your college years. Maybe you can't go into full-time ministry. Maybe you are unable to financially support Christian ministries as much as you could have in years past. But you can carry the message of Christ across the street. You can reach out to the needy people in your community with the love of Christ. You can help mold the lives of young people by serving in the children's ministry of your church. You can pray that God will open the hearts of those you know.

Don't worry, God will always have a Nineveh of some sort—some place where he can use your life for His glory and His kingdom. Turn back to God and give Him your total commitment. And remember the prophet Samuel's challenge to the Israelites before his death: "Be sure to fear the Lord and serve him faithfully with all your heart; consider what great things he has done for you" (1 Samuel 12:24, NIV).

eleven

A SECOND CHANCE
AFTER FAILURE

The third time he said to him, "Simon son of John, do you love
me?" Peter was hurt because Jesus asked him the third time,
"Do you love me?" He said, "Lord, you know all things; you
know that I love you." Jesus said, "Feed my sheep."
    JOHN 21:17, NIV

Is there a way back after we have failed God? Yes there is! And
perhaps no story from the Bible better illustrates that point than
the story of Peter's fall and the way Jesus recommissioned him
for service. It is a truly amazing story when you think about it.

Jesus had been deserted by His own followers at the time
of His deepest trial. How easily Jesus could have written them
all off and said, "You didn't stand by Me in My greatest hour of
need; now I'm not going to stand by you in yours." But no, the
Lord sought to restore them. After His resurrection we see the
risen Lord seeking out these discouraged, disheartened disciples and trying to revive them—to reignite their spiritual fire and
give them a second chance.

Perhaps the most notable of the resurrection appearances
would be the one to Simon Peter. This man really needed
encouragement. After all, he had denied and deserted the
Lord—something he said he would never do—and he was
devastated. His last picture of Jesus was on the cross, where he
saw a beaten, bloodied human frame that was hardly recogniz-
able. There hung his precious Lord, the One he had pledged to

131

stand by through thick and thin, and yet Peter had abandoned Him in His hour of need.

Peter was distraught. His world had come crashing in on him. And all that he held dear was now lying dead in a tomb. He had so many regrets. And he would never be able to tell the Lord he was sorry. This often happens to people when someone close to them dies. They think of their last encounter together and say, "I wish I could have told him how much I loved him one last time."

Often survivors feel guilty. Perhaps there was something they could have done to avert this person's death. Imagine how Peter felt in this lonely hour. The last glance of His Lord was one where he had just bitterly denied Him for the third time. He had even taken an oath of sorts, saying, in essence, "May God kill and damn me if I am not telling the truth; I never knew the man."

Then Peter saw the Lord. His pure, holy, all-knowing eyes pierced through him like the morning sun. He couldn't get that picture out of his mind. And then after Jesus was led away, Peter surely thought about what he could have done to stop it. But He hadn't. Sure, he had pulled out a sword and taken a wild swing in a feeble attempt to defend Jesus in the Garden of Gethsemane, but he knew full well he had miserably failed his Lord.

We could easily wonder why Jesus even chose Peter to be one of His disciples in the first place. It's important to know that when Jesus handpicked Peter, He knew exactly what He was doing. He knew this salty fisherman was made of tough stuff. There were no surprises for the Lord. He even knew that Peter would eventually fail. But Jesus deeply loved this man, just as He loves you and me. And He gave him a second chance.

When the women came back from the tomb where the crucified Lord had been laid and reported to the disciples that Jesus had risen, Peter and John had to see for themselves. They raced to the tomb and looked in. When John saw the cloth strips that had been wrapped around the Lord, he was convinced that the Lord had indeed risen from the dead. Peter, who arrived a few moments later and surveyed the exact same scene, walked away perplexed about what it all meant.

Interestingly, the angel who had spoken to the women at the tomb had told them specifically to "tell the disciples and Peter He is risen." Isn't that amazing? Here is the Lord through one of his holy messengers responding to the doubts of His beloved follower. The message was not, "Go tell the disciples and John He is risen," or "Go tell the disciples and Mary He is risen," or "Tell the disciples and Matthew He is risen." No, it was, "Tell the disciples and Peter He is risen," because Peter needed special reassurance.

Maybe something has happened in your life that has caused you to doubt God. Maybe you had a bad experience in church. Perhaps some minister or other person misrepresented God to you. My hope is that the same Jesus who restored Peter will also restore your faith.

Perhaps you need a second chance. Maybe there was a time in your life when you had a vibrant faith, but other things have crowded Christ out. Maybe it has been a series of sins you have gotten yourself into—a lifestyle you know is wrong. The same God that gave a second chance to His disciples, and especially Peter, is still giving them out today.

We know that Peter and His Lord had a personal encounter after this event. Scripture doesn't really elaborate, but one thing is clear: Peter was not only forgiven; he was also recommissioned to represent the Lord again. It is illustrated for us in John 21.

As the chapter begins, we see the disciples waiting around for something to happen. They were waiting in Galilee, as commanded by the Lord, but nothing had taken place. Boredom was apparently setting in, and it was Peter who said, "I'm going fishing!"

The others chimed in, "We'll go with you!"

So they loaded up their gear, boarded their boats, and went out just as in old times. It was the same crew that had spent so much time together. They could possibly have wondered whether things might go back to the way they had once been; that is, before Jesus came along and chose them to follow Him. But deep down inside they all knew that things would never be the same. Probably no one even wanted them to be. But what now? Where was Jesus? What was the next step? Had He forgotten about them? And, like old times, they pulled up empty nets.

How many times have you just wanted to leave your problems behind, hang a Gone Fishing sign on your office door, and just get away from it all? That's exactly what the disciples did. They fished. And they had the empty nets to prove it. That wasn't really a bad thing. Jesus had them catch nothing to prove a point: It is futile and useless for us to live without the direction and blessing of Jesus.

We can go out and catch nothing. We can aim at our goals. We can work hard in business—work hard at everything we hold dear—and still end up unfulfilled because we didn't allow the Lord to direct our life. We didn't invite Him to bless our plans, or more important, direct us in our plans. So often we think, *It's my life and my future and my career and my family and my money*. We forget that we belong to God.

This is especially true of Christians. For the Bible says, "You are not your own; you were bought at a price. Therefore honor God with your body" (1 Corinthians 6:19-20, NIV). But it's even true in the broad sense of any person living on this earth, Christian or not. We were all created by God. The very breath that we draw into our lungs is a gift from God. But we think that it is ours by right.

Life Is Not Always As It Seems

A lady was working very hard one day. She decided to take a little time off from her busy schedule for a lunch break. She thought to herself, *I am going to go and just spoil myself right now.* So she drove down to the local shopping mall. When she got there, she went straight to Mrs. Field's Cookies.

She said, "I want a full bag of hot chocolate chip cookies. And put some walnuts in them."

So they made up these fresh, hot, delicious cookies, and she ordered a tall glass of cold milk on the side. She walked over to a table, sat down, kicked off her shoes, and made herself comfortable. Then she opened up her purse, pulled out her newspaper, and thought to herself, *I'm just going to relax, read the paper, eat these delicious, just-out-of-the-oven cookies, and wash them down with cold milk.*

As she began to read the paper, she heard a little commotion. She looked over the top of her paper. The man sitting across from her reached into the little bag and took a cookie. She thought to herself, *That's odd. Why did he do that?* And she took a cookie out of the same bag. She thought he certainly wouldn't do that again.

She went back to reading her paper. He moved again. She pulled the paper down to look at him. She wanted to catch him in the act. He didn't seem ashamed. He reached in and took another cookie. He even smiled at her while he was eating it. She reached in and took a cookie, too. Then he reached in and took another as well. Then she took one more cookie, and so did he.

This went on until almost all of the cookies in the little bag were gone. She was getting angrier by the minute, thinking, *How can this man just sit there and take my cookies right in front of me and have the audacity to actually smile about it?*

There was only one cookie left. They both reached in at

the same time, but he got it first. He split the cookie and gave her half. She quickly snatched it away. She ate her half, and he ate the other.

Enraged, she jumped up from the table. She was fuming. Grabbing her newspaper, she quickly folded it and opened up her purse to put it away. There in her purse, much to her surprise, was her bag of cookies.

Things aren't always the way they seem. She thought that the man had been stealing her cookies when in reality she was stealing his. Yet he was so gracious. He even split the last cookie with her. She was so embarrassed.

We can be that way with God, too. "It's *my* life!" we fume; "*my* choice; *I'm* in charge!"

And the Lord is so gracious and loving. But we need to remember that it's *His* life. It's *His* future. He wants to guide and direct our steps. He has a custom-designed plan for our lives. We should say, "Lord, what do You want us to do? We want You to guide and direct our steps. We don't want to go fishing and pull up empty nets. We want You to direct us. We want You to guide us."

The fishing disciples didn't have God's direction at this particular time. As they were pulling up empty nets, they heard a voice calling from the shore: "Children, have you any food?" The Greek work for *children* could also be translated "boys." I prefer that translation, like a father talking to his sons. "Boys, did you catch anything?"

They might have been a little upset. "Who is He calling *boys?* We are full-grown, adult men." I don't think they were respectful when they responded. They didn't know who this guy was. "No. Don't rub it in," they answered.

Then the man from shore said, "Why don't you cast your nets on the other side of the boat, and you will catch a lot of fish!"

John, always the perceptive one, said, "It's the Lord. I can't make Him out. I can't see His features. But I'm telling you, it's the Lord." When they pulled up their nets, after listening to and obeying the Lord's direction, they had so many fish that their nets couldn't contain them all.

Why did Jesus ask them, "Do you have any food?" He wanted them to admit their failure—not to rub their faces in it, but to get them to acknowledge that they needed His help.

Today nobody wants to admit wrongdoing. We want to blame it on somebody or something else. We want to blame it on our circumstances or on some condition or *syndrome* that we claim to have. Nobody wants to say, "Yes, I am responsible." But Jesus wanted His disciples to come clean and call it what it was. Once they yielded to Him, they pulled up a large number of fish.

This scenario reminds us of a similar situation earlier in the disciples' ministry, recorded in Luke 5. They had fished all night and caught nothing. Jesus said, "Launch out into the deep and let down your nets for a catch" (v. 4).

They didn't really know the Lord all that well at that point. Peter, a veteran fisherman, replied, "Master, we've toiled all night and caught nothing!" (v. 5). He implied, "Jesus, we really appreciate You. We respect You. You are really the greatest teacher around. But, Lord, give us a little credit here. We are, after all, seasoned fishermen. We do this for a living, you know."

But it's interesting what Peter added: "Nevertheless at Your word I will let down the net." The phrase used could be translated, "At Your word, captain of this ship, we will do it." It's a unique nautical term not used any other place in the New Testament.

I wonder how that phrase was said. It makes all the difference in the world. Did Peter say it in respect and obedience? Or did he say it with sarcasm? Either way, when they followed the Lord's orders, they pulled up full nets, reminding them of how important it was to have Jesus on board, guiding and directing their steps.

When they brought the fish in to shore, they saw that the Lord had made a fire of coals, and fish were on it. Now this amazes me. The Creator of the universe, who had come to earth in human form, been crucified, and risen from the dead, was taking time to minister to even the smallest of needs of His disciples. He knew they would be chilled to the bone from being out on the cool water, so He built a fire.

Peter came in dripping wet, pulling the big net of fish. He walked over and stood in the fire's glow, probably embarrassed to even make eye contact with Jesus. For Peter, this was déjà vu. It had only been a short time since he had made eye contact with the Lord in the glow of a fire outside the house of Caiaphas. Now he was probably so humiliated, so ashamed, he could say nothing.

As they sat around the fire and ate, we don't read about anyone speaking. In the old days Peter might have been the first to speak up and perhaps boast of his deep love and devotion to the Lord. But he had no boasting to do that day.

Finally, Jesus broke the silence. He turned to Peter and said, "Simon, son of John, do you love Me more than these?" (v. 15). Note that He did not say Peter. He said Simon. Simon was the name given to him by his parents. Peter was the name Jesus gave to him, which means "rock." It speaks of solidity and strength. That day, however, Jesus saw Simon. In essence, Jesus was implying, "Hey, Simon, you haven't been acting much like a rock lately, have you?"

"Do you love me more than these?" Jesus asked. He only asked that particular question one time. It's true that He asked Peter three times, "Do you love Me?" But only one time did He ask, "Do you love Me more than these?" That's where His emphasis was.

The old Peter—the one in the upper room—would have said, "Of course, I love You more than these. Do fish swim? I would die for You." But the new, improved, humbled Peter only said, "Lord, You know that I love You." He had learned some important truths after he denied the Lord.

In the original rendition of this conversation, Jesus used the Greek word *agapao,* and Peter used the Greek word *phileo. Agapao* speaks of a sacrificial, deeply intense, all-out kind of love, whereas *phileo* speaks of a tender, affectionate, brotherly love.

In essence, Jesus asked Peter, "Do you love Me with an all-encompassing, devoted, and sacrificial love?"

And Peter replied, "Lord, I love You like a brother."

Or, putting it another way, Jesus said, "Peter, do you love Me 100 percent?"

And Peter said, "Lord, I can commit to 60 percent."

Simplifying it even more, Jesus asked, "Peter, do you love Me?"

And Peter responded, "Lord, I really like You a lot."

Now, I don't blame Peter for that. In reality, he did love the Lord, but no longer would he boast of his love for Jesus. That is always wise. Never boast of your love for God. Instead, boast of His love for you. Don't tell me how much you love Him, how much you have done for Him, what a wonderful servant you are. No. Tell how much He has done for you, how much He loves you, and all that He has worked out in your life.

A lot of people today run around saying, "Oh, I love Jesus so much!" But how do we really know if we love Jesus? Is it just a tender emotion that we feel inside, and if we cease to feel that emotion, does that mean that we no longer love Him? Or is there more to love than that? Of course, there is more, because love is more than a feeling. Love is a commitment that we make.

Earmarks of Those Who Love God

Let's close this chapter with five qualities that define those who really love the Lord. If we say we love the Lord, these earmarks should be evident in our lives:

1. *We will long for personal communion with God.* "As the deer pants for the water brooks," writes the psalmist, "so pants my soul for You, O God" (Psalm 42:1). "My flesh longs for You in a dry and thirsty land where there is no water. So I have looked for You in the sanctuary, to see Your power and Your glory" (Psalm 63:1-2).

If we really love the Lord, we will delight in worship and praise. If we really love the Lord, we will delight in the opportunity to gather together with God's people for fellowship—not out of duty, but out of desire. And so many of us miss out on so much when we fail to gather with God's people. Great blessings await those who obey God and fellowship with His people.

2. *We will love the things that God loves.* We know what He loves by what He has declared in His Word. "Oh, how I love Your law! It is my meditation all the day" (Psalm 119:97). It is amazing how our priorities change when we become committed Christians. Things that we never gave any thought to suddenly become so important. And things that used to be so important to us just fade away. We love the things that God loves—we love the Word, we love prayer, and we love fellowship.

3. We *will hate the things that God hates.* The Scriptures tell us in Psalm 97:10, "Let those who love the Lord hate evil, for he guards the lives of his faithful ones and delivers them from the hand of the wicked" (NIV). God hates sin. And we should too. The Bible tells us in Romans 12:9 to abhor what is evil and cling to the good.

So I love what God loves, and I hate what He hates. I hate to see the devastating power of sin wreaking havoc in the lives of so many.

4. *We will long for the Lord's return.* If we really love the

Lord, we will long for the return of Jesus. Paul rejoiced that in the future "there is laid up for me the crown of righteousness, which the Lord, the righteous Judge, will give to me on that Day, and not to me only but also to all who have loved His appearing" (2 Timothy 4:8).

5. *We will keep His commandments.* If we really love the Lord, we will keep His commandments, plain and simple. Love for Him is not merely some warm sentiment. Jesus said, "If you love Me, keep My commandments" (John 14:15). He also said, "Why do you call me 'Lord, Lord,' and not do the things which I say?" (Luke 6:46).

In his commentary on the Gospel of Matthew, Bible teacher John MacArthur points out that there is an engraving on a cathedral in Germany that beautifully reflects what Jesus is saying. Engraved on that cathedral are these words:

> Thus speaketh Christ our Lord to us: "You call me master and obey me not. You call me light and see me not. You call me the way and walk me not. You call me life and live me not. You call me wise and follow me not. You call me fair and love me not. You call me rich and ask me not. You call me eternal and seek me not. If I condemn you, blame me not.

If you really love God, it will show in your life.

"Do you love Me?" Jesus asked Peter. And He is still asking that question of us. "Do you love Me?" I wonder what our answer is.

Finally, Jesus said, "Feed My sheep" (John 21:17). For Peter that instruction was a recommission. Jesus was saying, "Peter, you are not finished. Not only have I forgiven you, but I'm going to use you in the days ahead. I'm recommissioning you. I'm giving you a second chance."

He is saying the same thing to us: "I'm giving you a second chance. I will give you another opportunity to walk with me and to be used for My service."

You might say, "But Greg, I have really failed. I've really blown it. I've sinned miserably. I'm not worthy."

Probably, but God will give you a second chance today anyway. He will forgive you for whatever you have done.

A SECOND CHANCE AFTER TRAGEDY

Praise be to . . . the God of all comfort, who comforts us in all our troubles, so that we can comfort those in any trouble with the comfort we ourselves have received.
2 CORINTHIANS 1:3-4, NIV

The phone rang. My heart sank when I heard the news. "Greg, you better come up to Riverside fast. Paul's daughter, Tobe, was struck by a car just in front of the church. It doesn't look good."

Paul Havsgaard is my assistant pastor at Harvest Christian Fellowship. That particular weekend, my wife and I had been on vacation. A friend was preaching that night, and Paul was holding down the fort in my absence. After the service, Tobe had tried to cross the street with a friend when tragedy struck.

It was night as she stepped into the crosswalk. She looked left but didn't look right, and she stepped into the path of a car driving approximately fifty miles per hour. I was an hour away, but I rushed as quickly as possible to the hospital. She was still holding on to life, and I wanted to pray with her and do what I could for the family.

I was numb with shock. I could still see Tobe's face in my mind and remembered her contagious smile, her buoyant personality, and her tender heart toward God. She was the same age as my son Christopher, and I had watched her grow up. I can still remember her as a little baby with her bright eyes and bubbly personality.

This vivacious fourteen-year-old had actively shared her faith at school. One day her dad found her crying in a secluded stairway at the church after a service. He gently approached her and asked her what was wrong.

"Dad," she said as tears streamed down her cheeks, "I'm thinking about all my friends at school who don't know Christ. I want them to know Him so much. I wish I could do more. I don't want them to go to hell."

Thinking about the potential loss of such a dynamic young lady with such a love for God and others seemed inconceivable. Why? I know many of us sitting up through the night in that hospital waiting room, though assured of Tobe's eternal destiny, still had that question ringing in our heads.

The surgeon who had operated on Tobe finally walked into the waiting room. We all looked carefully at his face, hoping for some sign of hope that little Tobe would pull through. Then he asked who the father was, and Paul identified himself. He asked Paul to describe what had happened when she crossed the street, which gave us a glimmer of hope that she was going to make it and the doctor merely needed some more information. He then asked Paul if he was indeed a pastor, and Paul said yes.

We wondered where this was all going. *What about Tobe?*

Finally, the surgeon said, almost casually, "Well, she didn't make it. We did what we could."

And that was it. I felt as though someone had punched me in the stomach full force. It was devastating. In all honesty I wanted to punch that doctor in the nose for the insensitivity with which he delivered the horrible news. Then again, this must be the hardest thing for a doctor to do. I could see he was just forestalling stating the painful truth.

Tobe was gone. I would never see her smiling face again or hear her bubbly voice—at least this side of heaven. What could I possibly say at such a moment? I felt the need myself to be comforted more than having the strength to comfort Paul and Kathy.

At that point something happened that I will never forget. Tobe's mother whispered aloud the words of a familiar praise song: "Give thanks with a grateful heart." What an amazing response! No screaming in agony, although we were all openly weeping. No outcries of protest to God. Just a grateful heart for the time that God had given her with Tobe. I knew at that moment that only God could have given Kathy that kind of strength and comfort as she faced the death of her precious daughter.

She was saying, "I don't understand it, Lord. But I give thanks to You. I cry out to You. I am dependent upon You."

Today, although Paul and Kathy still feel their loss deeply, and a day does not go by without their thinking of their dear Tobe, it is mixed with the joy of knowing that they will see their daughter again in heaven. But God has given them the opportunity to reach out to other bereaved parents with a ministry called The Lord Cares. They get the names of parents in the area who have lost their children. Then they invite them—Christian and non-Christian alike—to attend a monthly meeting at the church. There they identify with the parents' anguish, but they also bring real hope in a seemingly hopeless situation. They are living examples of the passage that says, "Praise be to the God and Father of our Lord Jesus Christ, the Father of compassion and the God of all comfort, who comforts us in all our troubles, so that we can comfort those in any trouble with the comfort we ourselves have received from God" (2 Corinthians 1:3-4, NIV). They can comfort with the same comfort they have received.

How different it is when we choose to harbor bitterness and blame instead of turning to the comforting presence of God. Consider the statistics for marital difficulties and divorce following the death of a child. Warren and David Wiersbe's book *Comforting the Bereaved* cites studies that "indicate that 90 percent of the bereaved couples have marital difficulties within a few months after the child's death."[1] Another group for bereaved parents, called The Compassionate Friends, states that approximately 75 percent of couples divorce within five years after the death of their child.[2]

What spiritual valley have you gone through in your life? Perhaps it was a time when unexpected circumstances suddenly came crashing down around you. Maybe it was a time when it even seemed as though God Himself had abandoned you. It could be that you are in the middle of some sort of hardship right now—a health problem, the loss of a loved one, or even a time of intense temptation and trial. It may be so hard that you are beginning to wonder if it's ever going to end.

Consider for a moment the familiar words of David concerning life's valleys in Psalm 23:4: "Yea, though I walk through the valley of the shadow of death, I will fear no evil; for You are with me; Your rod and Your staff, they comfort me."

David was no stranger to calamity and hardship. This man knew what it was like to suffer. He knew what it was like to face difficulties. He had been hunted like a wild animal by the paranoid king Saul, even after he had been anointed to be the next king of Israel by the prophet Samuel. When David wrote this psalm, which he penned under the direction of the Holy Spirit, he was brutally honest. By honest I mean that he not only spoke of the glory and power of God, but he also candidly revealed his own shortcomings, weaknesses, and questions that he faced in life. This psalm came from the school of hard knocks from a man who knew what it was like to need God's help.

Psalm 23 begins by looking at God's goodness to us. He leads us beside still waters. He takes us to green pastures. When we go astray, he puts us back on our feet. It could cause us to cry out in excitement, "Lord, You are so good to me! I will follow You wherever You go and do whatever You have in mind. I know it's good because I have come to recognize that the Shepherd's plan for me is better than my plan for myself."

The Lord might say, "Is that so? That's very good. I want you to go over here now."

"What's that, Lord?"

"It's called a valley."

"A valley? I don't do valleys, Lord."

"You want to follow me? Let's go to the valley."

"You know, Lord, I like mountaintops. I like for the sun to be shining. I like to hear the birds singing. I like good times. I really don't want friction or hardship."

But the Lord says, "You see that mountain in the distance?"

"Yes, I do! Isn't she a beauty? I would like to go there."

"The way to that mountaintop is through this valley."

"I'll tell you what, Lord. You go through the valley. I'll meet You on the mountaintop. If you would just airlift me from mountaintop to mountaintop, that would be wonderful."

"No," the Lord says, "you come with Me now through the valley."

We all go through valleys in life—hard times. They may be family problems or physical difficulties. They may be times of intense temptation or severe trials—or even the toughest of all problems, the loss of a loved one. Whatever the situation is, remember this: You are not alone. The psalmist says, "Yea, though I walk through the valley . . . I will fear no evil." Why? "For You are with me." God's presence is His great promise to the believer.

"But what if I don't sense His presence right now?" you may say. Imagine for a moment that it's an overcast day, and it's really cool. You don't see the sun. So you say, "The sun was here yesterday, but I don't see it today. I don't feel its warmth. Therefore, the sun must have gone away." The sun hasn't gone away; it's merely obscured by a cloud covering. If you don't believe that, go to the beach on a warm, overcast day and lie out without sunscreen protection. When you come home resembling a ripe tomato, you will realize that the sun was indeed out.

Similarly, when some people don't *feel* God, they falsely conclude that He is gone—that He has disappeared. But the truth is that He is there, even when we don't feel Him. And it's during these times that we must walk by faith, not by feeling. God has promised in His Word that He will be with us, and that is how we know He is always there.

Jesus says in Hebrews 13:5, "I will never leave you nor forsake you." In the great commission, He says, "Lo, I am with you always, even to the end of the age" (Matthew 28:20). And I love Isaiah 43:2, where God says, "When you pass through the waters, I will be with you; and when you pass through the rivers, they will not sweep over you. When you walk through the fire, you will not be burned; the flames will not set you ablaze" (NIV). Notice that God doesn't promise to keep you out of all trouble. He simply promises to be with you in the midst of it—even through death.

Death was never God's plan from the beginning. But now, because of the entrance of sin into the human race, all of us are going to die. Some will live longer than others, but eventually we are all going to die.

We think that the greatest tragedy is when someone dies young, like Tobe. I have performed many funeral services as a pastor. None of them is easy. Certainly when people are committed believers, it's glorious that I can talk about where they are and the lives they lived. It's hard when I'm not sure whether the person was a believer or not. But for me the hardest funeral is a child's funeral, especially if I knew the child. We think, *This is the ultimate tragedy—a small child dying.*

The funeral service I performed for Tobe Havsgaard was very difficult. And I'm not in any way saying it wasn't an extreme tragedy. But I don't think it was the ultimate tragedy. I think the ultimate tragedy is when a life has been lived to its entire length, wasted and squandered on sin.

I think of the words of Jim Elliot, a modern-day martyr of the faith, who was murdered along with four of his fellow missionaries in the Ecuadoran jungle as they tried to bring the gospel to the primitive Auca Indians. After a search party arrived at the scene of the massacre, Jim Elliot's journal was discovered with some of his personal thoughts and words. In his journal was this entry: "I seek not a long life, but a full one, like You, Lord Jesus." We think length of life is the ultimate, and it can be good to live long, but what's more important is to live right—to live a life that is full, right before God, and pleasing to Him.

It amazes me to watch people throw away their lives in the pursuit of selfish ambitions. Yes, it's sad when people die, but it's reality. And so is life beyond the grave.

Don't Carry Your Cares . . . Cast Them on Him
One of the surest ways to turn into a bitter, depressed person is to carry the weight of your grief and anguish on your own. God never meant it to be that way. When the Israelites were griping and complaining to Moses, he cried out to the Lord. When Hezekiah received a threatening letter from a king who was going to destroy him, he spread that letter out before the Lord. When John the Baptist was beheaded, his disciples went and told Jesus.

The point is, when trouble comes our way, we should cast it upon Him. Spread it out before Him. Call upon Him, "casting all your care upon Him, for He cares for you" (1 Peter 5:7). You don't serve and follow a God who is disinterested in your life. He is compassionate, concerned, and wants to help you.

Most of us would like to avoid the valleys of life, but there are some valuable lessons to be learned there that can be learned nowhere else. God reveals Himself in a unique and special way through the valleys of life. It's hard to believe now, but just remember this: Valleys don't last forever. First Peter 1:6-7 says, "In this you greatly rejoice, though now for a little while you may have had to suffer grief in all kinds of trials. These have come so that your faith—of greater worth than gold, which perishes even though refined by fire—may be proved genuine" (NIV). Trials don't last forever.

The psalmist David did not say, "Yea, though I crawl through the valley of the shadow of death." Nor did he say, "Yea, though I curl up and die in the valley of the shadow of death." He said, "Yea, though I walk through the valley . . ." Keep moving! You are going to get through it. There will be even greater mountaintops beyond, and you will learn great lessons and become more like the Good Shepherd. He will make you more compassionate, and He will show His strength in your weakness.

The World Is Watching

The world watches with great interest when Christians face hardship and adversity. Everybody faces hardships—we lose loved ones, we suffer sickness, we have financial reversals. But when it happens to Christians, unbelievers watch to see if our faith is genuine. They say, "Let's see how Mr. Christian acts now." That's our chance to show them what Christ can do even in hard times.

Acts 16:20-27 tells how Paul and Silas were thrown into prison for preaching the gospel. Their backs were ripped open with a whip. Yet, with their legs in shackles, spread as far apart as possible, causing excruciating pain, in the most unsanitary and filthy environment, Paul and Silas had a midnight worship service. They sang praises to God. Then an earthquake shook the prison, their shackles fell off, the walls came down, and they were free to go. You might say they brought the house down.

What's also amazing in this story is the reaction of the Philippian jailer. Seeing that the prisoners were now free, he knew he would be put to death. At that time if you were placed in charge of a group of prisoners and they escaped under your watch, you would not only be killed but tortured. So he took out his own sword, ready to kill himself.

Paul said, "Do yourself no harm, for we are all here" (v. 28).

And the next words out of the jailer's mouth were, "Sirs, what must I do to be saved?" (v. 30).

Paul and Silas had made an impact on that man's life. He must have thought, *Anyone who can sing praises to God in the condition these men are in, anyone who can praise God when his back is ripped open and his legs are in shackles—I want to know what makes him tick. Who is this God these men worship?*

Certain people are watching you right now, too. They are noticing how you behave. They are observing how you react to life. They want to know what you are all about—what kind of jokes you laugh at, what movies you go to see, what music you listen to, what you like to talk about. They are watching you—scrutinizing you. They may not let you know it, but they watch you quietly. And they are developing an opinion about God on the basis of your life.

A Christian is a letter written by God and read by other people. You are the only Bible some people are ever going to see. They are not going to read this book. They are going to look at your life. And that will determine the course their lives will take.

Are you in the midst of a trial right now that seems beyond your capacity to endure? Take it to the Lord. Don't keep it pent up inside. You have a choice about what you can do in response to tragedy. What you decide will affect your personal spiritual health and your witness for the Lord. Choose trust over turmoil and hope over hopelessness, knowing that God will see you through the valley.

God can also help you use your difficulties as tools to help others, as Paul and Kathy Havsgaard have done. Although our past experiences may have been particularly painful, we can be thankful that God can take our past and use it for His glory today. It's at that point we will discover that God can give us a second chance—a new beginning after tragedy.

A SECOND CHANCE
AFTER DEATH

This sickness is not unto death, but for the glory of God.
   JOHN 11:4

The story of the resurrection of Lazarus from the dead in John 11 gives us a unique insight into how God hurts with us when we are going through times of suffering. It also focuses upon one of the hardest problems to handle in the Christian life—when God doesn't do what we expect or want Him to do, when He doesn't answer our prayers our way, when He doesn't act the way we think He should act. Let's look now at John 11:1-15:

> Now a certain man was sick, Lazarus of Bethany, the town of Mary and her sister Martha. It was that Mary who anointed the Lord with fragrant oil and wiped His feet with her hair, whose brother Lazarus was sick. Therefore the sisters sent to Him, saying, "Lord, behold, he whom You love is sick."
>   When Jesus heard that, He said, "This sickness is not unto death, but for the glory of God, that the Son of God may be glorified through it."
>   Now Jesus loved Martha and her sister and Lazarus. So, when He heard that he was sick, He stayed two more days in the place where He was. Then after this He said to the disciples, "Let us go to Judea again."
>   The disciples said to Him, "Rabbi, lately the Jews sought to stone You, and are You going there again?"

Jesus answered, "Are there not twelve hours in the day? If anyone walks in the day, he does not stumble, because he sees the light of this world. But if one walks in the night, he stumbles, because the light is not in him." These things He said, and after that He said to them, "Our friend Lazarus sleeps, but I go that I may wake him up."

Then His disciples said, "Lord, if he sleeps he will get well." However, Jesus spoke of his death, but they thought that He was speaking about taking rest in sleep.

Then Jesus said to them plainly, "Lazarus is dead. And I am glad for your sakes that I was not there, that you may believe. Nevertheless let us go to him."

"Lazarus is dead." That is one of the most devastating statements we will ever hear. When we are waiting in the emergency room at 3:00 in the morning because someone we love is having surgery, and the doctor comes out with a grim look on his face, our stomach sinks and our mouth goes dry. And if he says our loved one is dead, it is devastating.

Doctors may use other terminology, such as *passed away*, or a clinical term like *expired.* But it all means the same thing. She died. And more significantly, she is gone.

We can feel as if our world has come to an abrupt end. Suddenly all of those things that were so important to us just hours ago—"Oh, I have to run those errands," or, "I have an appointment tomorrow"—now have no meaning at all. They become meaningless in the light of the loss of someone we dearly love.

Death is hard for everyone, even Christians. There is nothing wrong with feeling sorrow over the loss of someone we care about. It's part of the grieving process. Even the Bible says there is "a time to weep, and a time to laugh" (Ecclesiastes 3:4).

A young man named Stephen died a violent death for his

faithful proclamation of the gospel. He was a brave believer who heroically gave his life for the faith. After he died, the early believers wept over his body. They wept over the loss of this great light in the church. (See Acts 7:54–8:2.) Yes, death is hard. The death of Lazarus even brought tears to the eyes of Jesus. Yet, as Christians, we have the hope that we will one day be together again in heaven.

When God Seems Silent

As our story began, word was sent to Jesus that Lazarus was sick. Jesus was a friend of Mary, Martha, and Lazarus, who lived in the little village of Bethany, not far from Jerusalem. Jesus often spent time in their home. We know of at least one occasion when He had a meal with them.

If we had visited their home, Mary, Martha, and Lazarus could have rightfully said, "You know Jesus of Nazareth? He's our personal friend. We know Him. He comes by the house all the time! That's where He sat. Here's the plate He used." They were probably proud of His friendship. And I would be too. We all should be proud that He is our Savior, our Lord, and certainly our friend.

When these two sisters heard that their dear brother was ill, they probably thought, *No problem. We know Jesus. Send word to Him, and He will take care of it. He doesn't even need to come back. He will probably just say, "Lazarus, be healed," and it will happen simultaneously—right here in Bethany. Just send a message to tell Jesus that the one He loves is sick.*

It's interesting that it doesn't say, "Go tell Jesus that Lazarus is sick. Heal him." No, they said, "Just tell the Lord, 'Lazarus is ill.' There's no need to say, 'Heal him'; He will know." *He has a way of knowing these things*, they thought. They didn't even ask Him to come to visit them. They assumed that Jesus would speak a word and heal him. After all, they knew He had the ability, and they knew Jesus loved Lazarus. So, it was a done deal, right? Well, not necessarily.

God says, "My thoughts are not your thoughts, nor are your ways My ways. . . . For as the heavens are higher than the earth, so are My ways higher than your ways" (Isaiah 55:8-9). There are times when we do not understand what God is doing or why He is not doing more in a certain situation. So when the message about Lazarus reached Jesus, He said, "This sickness is not unto death." This statement didn't mean that Lazarus wouldn't die. As a matter of fact, Lazarus was already dead when the message arrived. The words of Jesus meant that death was not the final word.

We have heard the expression "It's a fate worse than death." We may wonder, *What could be worse than death?* But there are fates worse than death, such as where you spend eternity. Death is merely a mode of transportation, not the end. And when we board the last train of this life, we are either going into the presence of God in heaven or to be judged in a place called hell. It's not so much the trip that's the issue—it's the destination.

When Mary and Martha originally informed Jesus about their brother's illness, they most likely expected to see Lazarus recover as soon as the message reached Him. But nothing happened. Instead of coming immediately, the Lord intentionally waited for two more days, finally arriving in Bethany a full four days after Lazarus had died.

From this we learn that Jesus may be completely informed of our trouble, yet act as though He is indifferent to it. In other words, He may not do what we expect Him to do. We say, "Lord, excuse me. Are You paying attention here? We have a problem. What are You going to do about it?" But the comfort in prayer is not that Jesus always answers as we wish, because He doesn't. The great comfort is that He who makes and controls all circumstances knows what is best and will act accordingly. He will do the right thing.

We might say, "That's all fine and good for Lazarus. He's dead. Jesus shows up, and he's brought back to life. That's a story with a happy ending." But wait a second. As Christians, won't we be raised, too? The ultimate glory was not that Lazarus came back to life. In fact, it's kind of sad. How would you like to die and have to come back only to die again at a later date? Poor Lazarus had to die twice.

The message Mary and Martha sent was, "He whom You love is sick." The Greek word here for *sick* means "deathly sick." It was a critical problem. But Jesus waited. And they were no doubt thinking, *He is going to let us down. Maybe prayer doesn't work.*

Perhaps you have felt that way. You brought your need before the Lord: "God help me. I'm calling out to You." You have told all your friends, "God will come through for me. Jesus will take care of this. You just watch." Again you pray, but He doesn't answer your prayer the way you want Him to. So you're embarrassed—devastated. You might even think that Jesus doesn't love you anymore because, in your mind, He has let you down.

But look at John 11:5: "Now Jesus loved Martha and her sister and Lazarus." In the original language there's an interesting little twist that adds meaning to this story. When they said, "Jesus, he whom you love is sick," Mary and Martha used the Greek word *phileo*, which we've already seen means "brotherly love."

Later, when it says that Jesus loved Lazarus, Mary, and Martha, a different Greek word—*agapao*—is used, a word that you'll remember speaks of a sacrificial, agonizing love for a person in spite of that person's unlovability.

Phileo would say, "I want to be your buddy. And if you are nice to me, I will be nice to you. We like each other. We have similar interests and tastes. We get along. Let's be friends." But *agape* encompasses love for a person who is unlovable to you, who is unappealing, maybe even somewhat repulsive. *Agape* says, "I love you, no matter what."

Agape is the word used in John 3:16 where it says, "God so loved the world that He gave His only begotten Son." Jesus died for every person—for beautiful people and for unattractive people. And who is to say which is which? We all make those determinations in our lives, but God loves us in spite of ourselves—in spite of our unlovability. Jesus loved with a deeper love.

Here is the point: Mary and Martha said, "Your buddy is sick. Your friend is sick." Jesus said, "I have a love for you that is deeper than *phileo*, and I am going to do something for you that is greater." They only thought of friendship, but Jesus was thinking of sacrificial love. They were thinking of their temporal comfort; Jesus was thinking of their eternal benefit. They wanted a healing; He wanted a resurrection. He wanted to do above and beyond what they could ask or imagine.

We think the worst-case scenario is death. How could that possibly be the will of God? And that is a difficult question to answer as we dwell on this side of eternity. We don't see the big picture, because we are only interested in what benefits us temporarily. God is looking at the long term.

There are some things this side of heaven I am never going to understand. I don't have all of the answers. Sometimes people will say to me after a tragedy, "Greg, why did God allow this?" And instead of having to give some canned answer, many times I say, "I don't know. I just can't answer that, but I know this: God loves you. I know this: God is wiser than you. I know this: 'All things work together for good to those who love God, to those who are the called according to His purpose' " (Romans 8:28). When I don't know something, I fall back on what I do know. And it's hard, because it's during those times that we must walk by faith. We don't understand it. There is turmoil going on deep inside us, and we don't know what God has in store for us.

Perhaps you've had a setback in your life. Things were going well, and you were on a roll. Then whammo! You went down in flames—in business, in a relationship, or in some other area. So you said, "Excuse me, God, hello? What's this all about? How could this possibly result in anything good?"

I'm sure Joseph felt that way, too. He was a young man who was faithful to the Lord, but he had setback after setback and sank deeper and deeper into his problems. Each setback was actually a stepping-stone to a greater plan that God had in store for him, which resulted in his being used more powerfully by God. When all was said and done, he was able to tell the very brothers who had sold him into slavery, "You meant evil against me; but God meant it for good" (Genesis 50:20). Like Joseph, one day we may be able to look back and say, "Now I know why the Lord did this." For some of us, though, that may only happen on the other side of eternity.

In the same way, Jesus acted out of love for Mary, Martha, and Lazarus. He waited to come to Bethany because He loved Mary, Martha, and Lazarus. Then He went because He loved Mary, Martha, and Lazarus. For their sakes He waited, and for their sakes He went.

Some people would say, "That doesn't make any sense." Think of it this way: The same could be said of His return. He tarries or waits because of His love for sinners. The Bible says that God is "not willing that any should perish but that all should come to repentance" (2 Peter 3:9). He will return because of His love for His church.

Now let's look at John 11:17-26. Jesus is finally making His way back to Bethany.

So when Jesus came, He found that [Lazarus] had already been in the tomb four days. Now Bethany was near Jerusalem, about two miles away. And many of the Jews had joined the woman around Martha and Mary, to comfort them concerning their brother.

Now Martha, as soon as she heard that Jesus was coming, went and met Him, but Mary was sitting in the house. Now Martha said to Jesus, "Lord, if You had been here, my brother would not have died. But even now I know that whatever You ask of God, God will give You."

Jesus said to her, "Your brother will rise again."

Martha said to Him, "I know that he will rise again in the resurrection at the last day."

Jesus said to her, "I am the resurrection and the life. He who believes in Me, though he may die, he shall live. And whoever lives and believes in Me shall never die. Do you believe this?"

Martha was waiting impatiently for the Lord. She may have been fuming, "When is Jesus going to show up? He is so late. I can't believe He did this to us, His close friends!" Finally, there He is. She runs to Him and says, "Lord, if you had been here, my brother would not have died." It sounds to me as if Martha is scolding Jesus. Aren't you glad Jesus is patient with us? I'm so glad that God doesn't lose His temper, aren't you? A celestial temper tantrum is a frightening prospect to consider. Thank God it isn't a possibility. God is righteous. When He is angry—and He is angry on occasion—it's a righteous indignation. It's not the kind we experience when someone offends us and we want to pay him back. No, it's a righteous indignation with a purpose.

But you see, Jesus was tolerant. He understood that Martha was hurting. We have to give her credit—she was honest. She said what she was thinking, and she still believed in Him. She said, "Lord, if You had been here, my brother would not have died." She still trusted Him. And she still had confidence because she added, "But I know that whatever You ask of God He will give You."

I don't know whether Martha really believed what she said, because when Jesus said that Lazarus would live again, she said, "He's dead, Lord, and he stinks. He's decomposing." I don't think she was ready for what Jesus was about to do.

What I like about Martha is that people always knew where they stood with her. She was one of those ladies who spoke her mind. Remember in Luke 10:38-42, when Jesus came to their house for a meal, and Martha asked Him to tell Mary to stop sitting at His feet and help her in the kitchen? She wasn't happy and others were going to know about it. But Jesus answered, "Martha, Martha, you are worried and upset about many things, but only one thing is needed. Mary has chosen what is better, and it will not be taken away from her" (NIV). There is a time to work and a time to wait. There is a time to pray and a time to move. This was a time to sit and listen.

When Jesus Wept

The story in John 11 progresses and becomes even more dramatic in verses 32-39:

> When Mary came where Jesus was, and saw Him, she fell down at His feet, saying to Him, "Lord, if You had been here, my brother would not have died."
>
> Therefore, when Jesus saw her weeping, and the Jews who came with her weeping, He groaned in the spirit and was troubled. And He said, "Where have you laid him?"
>
> They said to Him, "Lord, come and see."
>
> Jesus wept. Then the Jews said, "See how He loved him!"
>
> And some of them said, "Could not this Man, who opened the eyes of the blind, also have kept this man from dying?"

Then Jesus, again groaning in Himself, came to the tomb. It was a cave, and a stone lay against it. Jesus said, "Take away the stone."

Martha, the sister of him who was dead, said to Him, "Lord, by this time there is a stench, for he has been dead four days."

In that time they did not have the embalming elements we have today. When a person died they wrapped the body in spices in sort of a mummylike enclosure. They didn't have formaldehyde or makeup to put on the deceased. Today, after the mortician is done, some people look better dead than when they were alive. They can do wonders, but without these modern capabilities Lazarus was clearly in the process of decomposition.

Jesus had raised the dead before, but He hadn't done so with anyone who had been dead as long as Lazarus. He raised up the child of Jairus quickly after her death. He raised up the son of the widow of Nain only a few hours after his passing. But Lazarus was very, very dead. He was beyond gone.

John 11:35 says simply, "Jesus wept." In verse 33 we read that others were weeping. They were mourning, but it was completely different from what Jesus did. The Greek word used to describe this weeping of Mary and the others could best be rendered "wailing." It was a moaning, wailing kind of grief. But that is not how Jesus wept. The Greek word used to describe how Jesus wept could be translated "tears were running down His face."

Jesus surveyed the scene. Mary, Martha, the people—everyone was wailing and moaning, and tears just rolled down His cheeks. Jesus wept. But why?

1. They were the tears of sympathy for Mary and Martha for all of the sorrow that is caused by sin and death. Jesus Christ was, according to the Bible, a man of sorrows and acquainted

with grief. He knows and understands the pain and hurt deep inside your soul when you have lost someone you love. Maybe people will never completely understand, but in that sense Jesus has wept with you as well.

2. They were tears of sorrow for Lazarus. Because he was dead? No, those tears were for one who had known the bliss of heaven and now would have to return to a wicked earth, where he would have to die again.

3. They were tears for the unbelief of the people. Jesus was not only surrounded by these people who were moaning and wailing but by Mary and Martha, who were unbelieving, too, in spite of what He had said: "I am the resurrection and the life. He who believes in Me, though he may die, he shall live. And whoever lives and believes in Me shall never die. Do you believe this?" (John 11:25-26).

John 11:33 says that Jesus was *troubled*. A better translation of that verse would be that He troubled Himself, and He was moved with indignation. To really simplify it, Jesus was angry. So we see Jesus weeping. Then we see a righteous indignation welling up within Him.

What brought on not only His sorrow but also His anger? The ravages of sin in the world He had created. He was angry. He might have been thinking, *Look at what sin has done to My creation. Look at how it has marred human existence.* Have you ever had something destroyed that you had invested a great deal of work on? Maybe you have been building a model ship for years. You go into model shops and see beautiful ships you can build with all the masts, materials, and little strings. If you commit to such a project, it can take months.

I have been building a few models lately. I guess I thought that as an adult I would be better at it than when I was twelve. It's sad to realize that I'm not. I still make the same mistakes. I get glue all over everything, and now they have superglue, which is the worst thing I could ever use. My fingers have been glued together more than once. What a mess.

Still, imagine working on something like that—applying so much effort to it—and then seeing it smashed before your eyes. Here was God's creation—His original plan now flawed by sin. Death was a part of the curse, and it angered Jesus to see the devastating effect it had on humanity.

We say, "Well, why doesn't He do something about it?" He has. And He will. He has by going to the cross of Calvary and dying for our sins so that death doesn't have to be the end. We can have life beyond the grave in a new body. And He will come again and establish His kingdom.

The conclusion of the story is found in John 11:40-44:

> Jesus said to her, "Did I not say to you that if you would believe you would see the glory of God?" Then they took away the stone from the place where the dead man was lying. And Jesus lifted up His eyes and said, "Father, I thank You that You have heard Me. And I know that You always hear Me, but because of the people who are standing by I said this, that they may believe that You sent Me." Now when He had said these things, He cried with a loud voice, "Lazarus, come forth!" And he who had died came out bound hand and foot with graveclothes, and his face was wrapped with a cloth. Jesus said to them, "Loose him, and let him go."

"Lazarus, come forth!" Only Jesus can call to the other side of eternity and be heard.

Lazarus was on the other side. He was probably just starting to get the lay of the land. "Let's see . . . the Great White Throne is over there. The glassy sea is over there. Things are looking good. I like this."

Suddenly a voice resonates, "Lazarus."

"What?"

"Come forth!"

"Oh no."

"Come back, Lazarus."

The same voice that spoke creation into existence was speaking beyond the veil that separates eternity from life on earth. And He called Lazarus back. Jesus had answered their prayers beyond their wildest imaginations. He gave Lazarus a second chance, even after death.

We, too, will one day hear the voice of Jesus call us forth from the grave, and we shall rise to meet Him in the air.

Our task in the meantime is to ensure that our families and friends are able to hear His call when it comes. We must call them forth from their graves of sin into a relationship with Him so that we can all rise together on that glorious day.

MAKiNG GOOD
ON YOUR
SECOND
ChANCE

part 4

A HUNGER
FOR HOME

*When he had spent all, there arose a severe famine in that land,
and he began to be in want.*
     LUKE 15:14

Have you ever been homesick? It's a natural feeling when we're
traveling on business and away from our families. It happens
when we go away to college. People in the service know what
it's like. We might hear a song on the radio that reminds us of
home. Maybe the cry of a baby makes us think about our young
children. Even a pleasant aroma—the perfume our wife wears
or familiar kitchen smells—can leave us longing desperately for
home.

     I know that feeling. It's especially tough for me when I'm
overseas. Not only am I looking forward to being reunited with
my family, but I miss my country. I miss America. I appreciate
understanding the language and all of its nuances. I get so tired
of trying to figure out what people are saying to me and about
me when I'm in a foreign land. It's also just great to wake up in
your own bed. There are certain foods I absolutely crave from
back home as well.

     A few times on trips overseas I've been offered some
pretty weird food—some I didn't find exactly appetizing. For
instance, in the Philippines a few years ago they wanted to
serve me something called *baloot*. It is considered a great deli-
cacy in that nation. It's basically a duck egg with a little duck-

ling partially formed inside. Part of it resembles the substance of a hard boiled egg, surrounded by a brown fluid. When they serve it, they open the top of the shell to expose that little duck head. They eat it, then they drink the fluid. They think it's delicious. To each his own.

One night I was dining with a group of missionaries in a home. The hosts wanted to serve me some baloot.

"Greg, we want to honor you and serve you baloot," the host announced proudly.

"Oh, you know, I'm not very hungry," I said. "Thank you."

"Oh no, you don't understand," I was told by someone sitting next to me. "It's a great honor."

"I appreciate that, but I really couldn't."

Someone whispered in my ear, "You better eat it, or they will be culturally offended."

I whispered back, "You know what? If I eat it and then proceed to throw up, they will be even more culturally offended. And I know that is exactly what would happen." So I didn't eat the baloot.

My friend Mike had a similar experience. He was in a country where the greatest part of the meal was when they served the actual head of the bird, which I believe again was a duck. Mike has sort of a weak stomach and doesn't like exotic food. His idea of exotic cuisine is a little ketchup on a hamburger. But he was famished and looking forward to dinner.

After everyone at the table was given a serving of duck, Mike was given his portion under a silver cover. He was so hungry that he could hardly wait. They placed the platter in front of him, pulled off the cover, and there it was—a duck's head, staring right at him. He was immediately nauseated, but he politely said, "I'm afraid I'm not really very hungry. I don't have any appetite."

Later, he went up to his room and waited for everyone to go

to bed. He called down to the kitchen and said, "Quick, send me up a sandwich. I'm starving to death." Up came a platter. He eagerly lifted off the lid, saw a sandwich waiting for him, and picked it up. As he was preparing to take a huge bite, he pried open one corner to see what kind of sandwich it was. You guessed it—it was the duck's head again. They had saved it for him!

Yes, it's great to get back to your own home—to the good old USA. It's familiar. It's comfortable. It's home, and there's no place like home, as Dorothy said in *The Wizard of Oz*. But in a sense I think each of us, as a child of God, has a certain homesickness for our spiritual home in heaven. Have you ever felt like nothing in this life could completely satisfy the deepest needs of your heart? That feeling is a homesickness for heaven.

One day a family's pet cat named Clem disappeared. After a while, his owners sadly concluded they would never see Clem again. Eight years later, they heard a scratching noise at their door. They opened it and in walked a cat they didn't think they had ever seen before. He climbed up into Clem's favorite old chair and started purring as if he owned the place. They thought, *Could this be Clem?* They found old photographs of their cat from eight years before, compared them to the cat that was in the chair, and sure enough it was Clem. How did he find his way home? Where had he been? What kept him away? No one will ever know. But he had some kind of homing instinct and found his way after a long time.

We see that homing instinct in many animals. In southern California, where I live, there is a place called San Juan Capistrano, home of a famous Spanish mission where the swallows return every year. Thousands of tourists flood the area to witness this amazing sight of the swallows coming back to Capistrano. These birds have programmed in them the intuitive knowledge of returning to this area every single year.

Maybe it would be good if we had that kind of homing

instinct—an ability to find our way back to God when we're lost. We sometimes have that feeling of longing for something more, but we don't always know what to do about it. That is peculiar to the human condition. We're homesick for heaven.

Did you ever set goals for yourself when you were young? Did you ever think of what it would take to make you happy? You might have thought, *I know I will be happy when I get a house with a car in the garage and I am married with 1.2 children. That will do it.* Then you get the house and the car and the spouse and the children, and you're not satisfied, not by a long shot. You think, *Maybe if I just had a bigger house and a couple more children and two cars then I would be happy.* Yet when you achieve that, there is still something missing. What is it?

The Bible says that "God has put eternity in [our] hearts" (Ecclesiastes 3:11). That means that deep inside of us there is a longing, a hunger, for something more. There is a spiritual drive. Why? Because you and I were created to know God. Think of it this way: There is a God-shaped vacuum in the heart of every person, regardless of age, race, gender, or station in life. We as humans, created in the image of God, have a drive to rise above the commonplace, the ordinary.

A quick look through the *Guinness Book of World Records* shows how so many have tried so hard to distinguish themselves. For instance, Jesse Owens holds the record for the most Olympic track records in a day. The longest reigning heavyweight boxing champion was Joe Louis, who held the title for almost twelve years. The oldest boxing champion was George Foreman, who was forty-five when he knocked out Michael Moorer to win the heavyweight championship in November 1994.

Others are known for their achievements in music. The most successful recording artist of all time is Elvis Presley, who had more than 170 hit singles and 80 top-selling albums starting in 1956. But the most successful musical group of all time is the Beatles, with more than a billion discs and tapes sold. The biggest seller of any record to date is "White Christmas" written by Irving Berlin and recorded by Bing Crosby. It has sold more than 170,884,207 copies.

The richest man in the world, Bill Gates of Microsoft Corporation, is worth an estimated $12.9 billion (and rapidly growing). Others are known for unusual achievements. One woman from India, for instance, wanted to be known for having the longest hair. Her hair measured thirteen feet ten and a half inches as of February 21, 1994.

Or there is the fastest talker. Few people are able to speak articulately at a sustained speed greater than 300 words per minute. But Steve Woodmore of Orpington, England, spoke 595 words in 56.1 seconds, or 637.4 words per minute, on the British television special "Motormouth" on September 22, 1990.

Others are known for more dubious achievements, such as the case of the gopher-hunting janitors of Fowler Elementary School in Ceres, California. They were alerted to the fact that a gopher was in the building. The three janitors cornered the animal in a utility room. Jeff Davis explained that he and his colleagues proceeded to spray the rodent with several canisters of a solvent used to remove gum from floors, hoping to freeze it to death. As one janitor lit a cigarette in the poorly ventilated room, sparks from the lighter ignited the solvent. A huge explosion blew all three out of the room and injured sixteen students. The gopher survived the incident and was released in a field.

As humans, we all have built into us the desire to achieve something—to make a mark, to distinguish ourselves. We all want our life to count for something big, and this desire for greatness is not in itself wrong. In Romans 2:6-8 we are told: "God 'will give to each person according to what he has done.' To those who by persistence in doing good seek glory, honor and immortality, he will give eternal life. But for those who are self-seeking and who reject the truth and follow evil, there will be wrath and anger" (NIV). Paul was approving those who do good, "seek glory, honor and immortality." God essentially wired us this way. It's built into us.

Before we consider man's purpose and place, let's briefly consider the question "Why did God create man?" Some have suggested that after creating our world and animal life, God found Himself lonely; so He created man. That's a sweet sentiment, rather heartwarming, and makes us feel really good about ourselves, but it's simply not true. I don't mean to burst anyone's bubble, but God would have personally done just fine without humanity. He is independent of humanity. God doesn't need the rest of creation for anything. If He created people to be personally happy or complete, that would mean He is dependent on us for that, which He isn't.

Paul summed up this concept in his message on Mars Hill when he said, "The God who made the world and everything in it is the Lord of heaven and earth and does not live in temples built by hands. And he is not served by human hands, as if he needed anything, because he himself gives all men life and breath and everything else" (Acts 17:24-25, NIV). The implication is that God doesn't need anything from humanity. God asked Job, "Who has given to Me that I should repay him? Whatever is under the whole heaven is Mine" (Job 41:11, NASB). No one has ever contributed to God anything that did not first come from God, who created all things.

Yet, though it is true that God didn't create us because He needed us or because He was dependent on us, it's also true that He created us for a special purpose, and we can bring joy to Him (and a wonderful by-product to ourselves). Don't think that because God doesn't *need* us He doesn't *want* us or that our lives are meaningless. He is intensely interested in our lives. He deeply and tenderly loves us beyond our comprehension, not because He had to (out of need), but because He chose to (out of love). He takes special delight in us above all other creations.

Scripture tells us, "The Lord your God in your midst, the Mighty One, will save; He will rejoice over you with gladness, He will quiet you with His love, He will rejoice over you with singing" (Zephaniah 3:17). Yet what does it mean when it says that we, as humans, are made in the likeness and image of God?

1. *Morally we are created in His image.* Humans (even fallen ones) have a sense of right and wrong. Paul tells us that even unbelievers "show the work of the law written in their hearts, their conscience also bearing witness, and between themselves their thoughts accusing or else excusing them" (Romans 2:15).

In contrast, this is not true of the animal kingdom. Although capable of incredible things and an impressive range of emotions, animals are not born with an innate sense of right and wrong. When we train them, they largely respond to the fear of punishment or the hope of reward. We can go to Sea World and watch Shamu, the killer whale, perform along with dolphins and other animals. Yet when these animals do their tricks, like jumping through a large hoop or waving to the audience with a flipper, it is not about being good or moral. They do it for a reward. As Shamu performs his great feats, something along the lines of *Do what it takes to have fish. Many fish!* goes through his mind. We like to attach human characteristics to animals, but they see things far differently.

2. *We have the ability to reason and think logically.* It's been said we use only 10 percent of our mental abilities. But even at 10 percent, we are far above the animal world. Animals can sometimes exhibit remarkable behavior in solving mazes, but they don't engage in abstract reasoning. There are no books called *The History of Canine Philosophy*, or *Why Can't There Be More Cheese? Deep Thoughts and Intellectual Musings from the Rat World*, or *Life in the Fishbowl: The Untold Story* by Charlie

Tuna. Nothing has changed among the animals, no mental advances have taken place. Beavers still build the same kinds of dams they have always built. Birds still build the same kinds of nests, and bees still build the same kinds of hives.

Meanwhile, humans continue to develop greater skills and complexity in technology, agriculture, science, and nearly every field of endeavor. If my dog wants water, he may attempt to communicate that by looking at his water dish. But he doesn't improve over time by building a sophisticated piping system into the yard. Perhaps our most significant ability as humans made in the image of God is that we can create. The incredible advances in technology in the last century are astounding. Our magnificent contributions in music and art are almost unbelievable.

I was created by God with an express purpose in life. To put it in a nutshell, I was created to give glory to God. God Himself tells us, "Everyone who is called by My name, whom I have created for My glory; I have formed him, yes, I have made him" (Isaiah 43:7). Along these same lines, Paul writes, "In Him also we have obtained an inheritance, being predestined according to the purpose of Him who works all things according to the counsel of His will, that we who first trusted in Christ should be to the praise of His glory" (Ephesians 1:11-12). Therefore, we are to glorify Him in all that we do with our lives.

Paul tells us, "Whatever you do, do all to the glory of God" (1 Corinthians 10:31). He also writes in 1 Corinthians 6:19-20, "Or do you not know that your body is the temple of the Holy Spirit who is in you, whom you have from God, and you are not your own? For you were bought at a price; therefore glorify God in your body and in your spirit, which are God's." Until we personally discover this great truth, we will walk through life aimlessly, without real purpose or meaning for our existence. If we fulfill the primary purpose God created us for, we will find as a by-product what most of us are looking for in life—happiness, purpose, and meaning. For Jesus said, "I have come that they may have life, and that they may have it more abundantly" (John 10:10).

The psalmist tells us of God's plan and purpose: "In Your presence is fullness of joy; at Your right hand are pleasures forevermore" (Psalm 16:11). When we realize that God created us to glorify Him, and we start to act in ways that fulfill that purpose, then we begin to experience an intensity of joy and fulfillment in the Lord that we have never known before.

This is why the story of the Prodigal Son that Jesus told is so very important. Certainly it's more than a story to help us with our earthly family lives. Clearly, He intended to give us a picture of what God is like and how He thinks about us as His children. This young man left his father, just as so many of us turn our backs on God. Soon he was beginning to see the emptiness of a life without his father. If this story took place today, the son would probably be calling home and asking his dad to wire him some more money. If the dad was smart and loved his son, he would refuse to underwrite his rebellion and sin.

Some people do the same with God. As they are living in sin they think they can ask God for His help or His blessing. Guess what? They don't receive it. The psalmist says, "If I regard iniquity in my heart, the Lord will not hear" (Psalm 66:18). God loves us too much to bless us and answer our prayers when we are living in sin.

Many people go out and break God's commandments, then wonder why He is not blessing them. Some are sexually involved outside of marriage. Others are stealing. Or maybe they are engaged in alcohol abuse or drugs. Whatever it is, they wonder, *Why is God not blessing my life?* The answer is simple: Because they are living outside of His will. Until they acknowledge their sin and turn from that lifestyle, they will never experience the full blessing of God in their lives.

Why is that? Does God like to discipline us? No, it's because He loves us. God doesn't want us to keep sinning. He knows we need to be uncomfortable if we're ever going to change. He wants us to be miserable for our own good, to come to our senses like the Prodigal Son and say, "I need to go home." Why did the Prodigal Son decide it was time to go home? He made two important discoveries—discoveries that we, too, can make about our relationship with our heavenly Father.

First, he realized that everything he needed was in his father's house. In Luke 15:17 he says, "My father's hired servants have bread enough and to spare, and I perish with hunger!" In other words, he says, "You know, the guys who just work for my dad are doing better than I am, the very son of my father." He realized how crazy that was. He saw that they had something he didn't have.

How does that apply to our longing to get back to God? One of the most attractive things about the Christian life is the lifestyle. People who are not believers are watching us. They are looking at the way we live. In fact, I didn't come to know Christ because someone took the time to share the gospel with me. I really can't remember that happening. Maybe Christians took one look at me and said, "Forget him. He would never believe." But I was attracted to the faith by watching the committed Christians on my high school campus. They were very active, confident, and outspoken. They would get together before school for prayer. They would unashamedly carry their Bibles around with them. They hugged each other after classes, even when they were only separated for forty-five minutes. They seemed to have a great time—a sense of family, community. And they seemed to care.

I saw real brotherhood in those Christians, camaraderie and real love. That intrigued me. It got my attention and made me listen to their message. Similarly, the Prodigal Son took notice of what others were experiencing.

Jesus told us that Christians are to be both salt and light in this world. He said, "Let your light so shine before men, that they may see your good works and glorify your Father in heaven" (Matthew 5:16). But we are also to be salt. What does that mean? Among other things, salt stimulates thirst. Most movie theaters have discovered this. Have you ever noticed how big the tubs of popcorn are in theaters? You can tell them you would like some popcorn, and the next thing you know they bring out something that looks like a five-gallon trash can. You haul it back to your seat and begin eating your overpriced, heavily salted popcorn. A few minutes later you're back at the counter looking for something to drink. They know they've got you because salt stimulates thirst. Likewise, your godly life will stimulate a spiritual thirst in others.

What did the Prodigal Son want out of life? Judging from his lifestyle, it seems to me that he wanted nice clothes, good food, and parties. What happened when he came home? His father gave him beautiful new clothes, he killed the fatted calf for dinner, and he said, "Let's have a party." In other words, everything he wanted in life was right there in his father's house.

It is the same way for us in our relationship with God. We don't have to go out into this world to find what we need. We will only find cheap imitations out there. We want love? Satan will offer us lust. We want a relationship with God? The world will offer us religion. We want peace? The world will offer us a drug-and-alcohol-induced haze. Cheap imitations. Why settle for those when we can have the real thing as a result of knowing the real God? Everything we need is in our Father's house.

The Prodigal Son went home for a second reason, too. Was it because he had shamed his father and wanted to make it right? I don't think so. Was it because he missed his older brother? Definitely not. Was it because of pangs of conscience? I don't think so. It wasn't his heart that drove him home; it was his stomach. He went home because he was hungry. He said, "I perish with hunger" (Luke 15:17). He wanted to eat.

Why do people come to Christ? Is it because they realize they have offended a holy God? Not usually. Is it because they realize they have broken His commandments and are sorry? Not very often. Is it because they know they have hurt God? No. People usually come to God for the same reason that the Prodigal Son went home—they are hungry, spiritually hungry. They realize that something is missing in their lives. They are empty, lonely, and afraid. They are looking for purpose, meaning, and hope in life. How easily God could turn us away for such an impure motive. Instead, He welcomes us with open and loving arms.

If we want to get right with God, we need to see the same things. We need to realize that everything we need in life is found in a relationship with God. There is nothing we need that God cannot provide.

Even if we don't have the highest motives, if we truly come to Jesus Christ, He will accept us. He will receive us and forgive us. In time we get the bigger picture of higher motives and how we were separated from God by sin.

Some people would criticize me for saying that. They might say, "The problem is you preach a human-centered gospel. You tell people that Jesus can fill the emptiness in their lives—that He can give them peace. What you really ought to say is, 'You have offended a holy God and sinned against Him. You have to turn away from sin and repent.' " I don't disagree with that statement. It's true that we have offended a holy God. And when I present the gospel, I emphasize that. But if we only say that to most people, we fail, because they couldn't care less about a holy God they have offended. However, people do recognize that they have voids in their lives. When we tell them that Christ can fill these voids, that appeals to them.

I am, after all, only following the example of my Lord.

Remember how He went to the woman at the well who had been married and divorced five times? She had lived an immoral life and was left all alone. I don't read that Jesus pulled out His soapbox, climbed up on it, and shouted condescendingly, "Hey you, harlot! You have offended a holy God. You have broken His commandments." What He said was, "Woman, if you drink of your water, you will thirst again. But if you drink of My water, you shall never thirst again" (see John 4:6-15).

Yes, it's true we have sinned against God. Yes, it's true that we deserve His judgment. But God appeals to our needs and offers to fill the void in our lives. After we come to Him, we have a better understanding of all the things that we have done and all the things that He has done. Jesus said, "I am the bread of life. He who comes to Me shall never hunger, and he who believes in Me shall never thirst" (John 6:35).

At the same time, we need to know that we have sinned against God—that we have offended Him. Unless we come to Him, we will, according to the Bible, face a certain judgment. To get right with God, we have to utter three very difficult words: "I have sinned." We don't like to use the word *sin* anymore. We prefer to say, "I am sick," or "I am dysfunctional," or "I have a disease." The truth is, we have sinned. It's hard for people to say that. It's especially hard for men to say it. We men feel we should always be in control. We think we can take care of ourselves. We are, after all, men! But we, too, have sinned. We need God's help. Everyone does—every man and woman—every single one of us. We have to say those three words: "I have sinned."

The Prodigal Son could have repeated his resolution every single day. "One of these days, I am going to say, 'Father, I am no longer worthy to be called your son.' I am going to go back home and get things right. Yes sir, I'll do that one of these days." In the same way we can say, "One of these days I am going back to church and get right with God." Yet it's not enough to simply recognize the problem. It's not enough to realize we are sinners. It's not enough even to see that Jesus died for our sins and offers forgiveness. We have to act on it. We have to get up and go to God. How tragic it would be to only talk about it yet never act on it. A. W. Tozer once said:

> The man who dies out of Christ is said to be lost, and hardly a word in the English tongue expresses his condition with greater accuracy. He has squandered a rare fortune and at the last he stands for a fleeting moment and looks around, a moral fool, a wastrel who has lost in one overwhelming and irrecoverable loss, his soul, his life, his peace, his total, mysterious personality, his dear and everlasting all."[1]

Don't let that happen to you. It's time to come home. Do it soon. Get home before dark. Your Father is waiting.

f i f t e e n

THE POWER OF
CONFESSION

He who conceals his sins does not prosper, but whoever
confesses and renounces them finds mercy.
        PROVERBS 28:13, NIV

When we want to understand a subject, the best thing to do is
find an expert—someone who has far-reaching firsthand experience. We don't often think of him this way, but Israel's King
David, the author of most of the book of Psalms, was just such
an authority on forgiveness and second chances. David was a
man of great power in another age and another culture.

For though David is rightfully known as one of the most
outstanding people of God in the pages of Scripture, identified
uniquely as a man after God's own heart, it is also true that
David was one of the greatest sinners in the Bible. His life, like
so many of ours, was a paradox. On one hand, we remember
him for his heroic exploits and his tender heart toward God and
others. On the other hand, we remember him for his sin of adultery and, in his attempt to cover it up, his sin of murder.

There are two ways, as David discovered, to approach sin:
We can either confess it, turn from it, and know the happiness
of being forgiven; or we can try to conceal it, be tormented by
it, and eventually have it found out anyway. David waited for
his sin to be found out. But he got his second chance because,
once caught, he confessed his sin and repented. He allowed
God to transform his life.

Unfortunately, there's a danger in waiting. We can't always count on getting that opportunity in this lifetime. That's why it is imperative to act immediately. There are no guarantees that there will be a tomorrow for us on this planet.

In Deuteronomy 30:19 God poses a challenge to us. He says, "I call heaven and earth as witnesses today against you, that I have set before you life and death, blessing and cursing; therefore choose life, that both you and your descendants may live." "Choose life," God is saying. "You can walk *with* Me, or you can walk *away* from Me. You can live, or you can die." It's amazing that some people consciously choose death. But that is what we do when we choose to sin over doing what God's Word says.

Granted, sin can be very attractive at times. The devil is no fool—he knows how to package his wares. You might even say he's something of a marketing genius. He knows how to present sin so it will have a certain appeal. Because of the short-term pleasure sin offers, many people don't think about its long-term repercussions.

Once you have what you lusted after, chances are it isn't what you imagined. Sin never is what it promises. It's largely hype. The few short-lived pleasures it can bring come at a tremendous cost, if not now, then later. And make no mistake about it, the Bible warns us that our sin will find us out. Sometimes it happens immediately; sometimes it happens after a period of time; but it always happens. It's inevitable, as David learned.

When we think of David, his name is usually paired with one of two others—Goliath or Bathsheba. Interestingly, in a broad sense, those two names sum up David's life. Goliath, the nine-foot-six-inch giant he courageously killed in the Valley of Elah, represents his greatest victory. His involvement with Bathsheba represents his greatest defeat.

While David triumphed over Goliath as a young man, his encounter with Bathsheba came later in life. The account in 2 Samuel 11 tells us that King David was walking on his rooftop at the back of the palace. The Bible says it was the time when kings went out to battle. General Joab was leading the troops into conflict, but David decided to stay home for a little rest and relaxation. From his rooftop terrace, he spied a beautiful woman named Bathsheba bathing. As king, David had extraordinary power over people's lives. So he had Bathsheba summoned to the palace. When she got there, David had sexual relations with her and later learned that Bathsheba had become pregnant.

Like most sinners, David didn't want people to know what he had done. Had he acknowledged his sin at this point, he could have limited the damage done, not only to his own life, but to other lives as well. Instead of repenting and coming clean, David believed he could use his kingly power to cover up his sin.

Bathsheba was married to a man named Uriah, who was off fighting in the war under General Joab. When Uriah got back from the front, he was summoned to the palace. Uriah, not knowing that David was involved with his wife, probably wondered, *Why am I being summoned to the king's palace? Why would I be asked to meet this great leader of Israel—the man after God's own heart? Imagine, he wants to meet me!*

"Uriah, good to see you," David may have said when they met. "Listen, you have been out there in battle for a long time. Why don't you go home tonight and be with your wife. Have a nice night. Go have a good time." David was hoping that if Uriah slept with his wife, then he would accept the child in her womb as his own. But David found out that instead of going home to be with his wife, Uriah slept that night at the palace entrance with the king's servants. Apparently, he couldn't think of enjoying himself while his fellow soldiers were out on the front lines risking their lives.

David must have thought, *Great, I have a do-gooder on my hands. Just what I need.*

The next night David called Uriah into his palace and got him drunk. Then he sent him home thinking the alcohol would overcome his character and inhibitions about enjoying himself with his wife. But Uriah again chose not to sleep with his wife.

Then David's tactics changed. He said, "All right, Uriah, go back to the front lines and take this message to Joab, my general." It was a message sealed with the signet of the king. Uriah did not dare think about opening it. He took it to Joab and proudly presented it saying, "The king wants you to read this." Joab opened the document from the king. It ordered the general to have Uriah lead his army into battle. Once engaged, the army was to pull back, leaving Uriah alone to die at the hands of the enemy. In essence, Uriah had delivered his own death sentence to Joab.

I wonder what Joab thought when he read the order. *My king is an interesting fellow—this "man after God's own heart." How could he do this? Why does he want this poor man dead?* But Joab obeyed his king. Off the troops went with Uriah leading the charge—a great hero. The troops retreated, and Uriah was killed.

Knowing Bathsheba was now a widow, David took her to be his wife. With all of his scheming and covering up, it looked as if David had pulled off a foolproof plan. It looked as if he had covered all of his bases. In fact, it even looked as if he had literally gotten away with murder. But there was something he forgot about—the God-instituted law of reaping and sowing. Not only does Scripture tell us that we will reap what we sow (see Galatians 6:7), but it also says our sin will find us out (see Numbers 32:23). The cover was about to be blown for this self-confident king.

David smugly covered his sin for a long time. Then one day the prophet Nathan came to him and said, "King, I have a problem, and I need to talk to you."

David was no doubt feeling quite regal sitting on his royal throne. He looked at the prophet and said, "Speak on."

"All right, Your Majesty. There were two men in one city. One man had many sheep. His neighbor had but one little ewe lamb. In fact, it was a family pet. When a visitor came to see the rich man, he was reluctant to kill one of his own flock. Instead, he decided to slaughter the one little ewe lamb that belonged to his neighbor. Your Highness, what do you think should be done to such a man?" asked Nathan.

As King David sat there he could feel the anger begin to rise. His blood was red hot with vengeance, and with all the royal fury he could muster he said, "This man should be put to death, and he should restore fourfold for the lamb!"

Now this was a very harsh sentence. Under Mosaic law, this type of violation wouldn't require the death penalty. What the fictional rich man had done was wrong, but it didn't merit death. But the self-righteous and judgmental David was ready to kill the man.

Then Nathan pointed his finger in the king's face and said, "You are the man!" (2 Samuel 12:7).

Suddenly, like being struck with a sledgehammer, David's fortress of deception, so carefully crafted, came crashing to the ground. In a flash it dawned on him that he had done exactly what the man with many sheep in Nathan's story had done. He had taken Uriah's wife when he had many wives of his own (in disobedience to God, by the way).

Nathan added, "The sword shall never depart from your house" (v. 10).

Yes, it took awhile, but David reaped what he had sown. His sin had found him out. But thank God for second chances. David learned from this experience. The story of David and Bathsheba serves as a backdrop to what David wrote in Psalm 32:1-7):

Blessed is he whose transgression is forgiven,
Whose sin is covered.
Blessed is the man to whom the Lord does not impute iniquity,
And in whose spirit there is no deceit.

When I kept silent, my bones grew old
Through my groaning all the day long.
For day and night Your hand was heavy upon me;
My vitality was turned into the drought of summer. Selah.
I acknowledged my sin to You,
And my iniquity I have not hidden.
I said, "I will confess my transgressions to the Lord,"
And You forgave the iniquity of my sin. Selah.

For this cause everyone who is godly shall pray to You
In a time when You may be found;
Surely in a flood of great waters
They shall not come near him.
You are my hiding place;
You shall preserve me from trouble;
You shall surround me with songs of deliverance. Selah.

The first question most people ask after reading that passage is, "What does *selah* mean?" Good question. Whenever we see that word after a stanza, we might want to go back and reread it. It's a way for the author to emphasize what he's writing—a way to underline it. Many of the psalms were actually songs. When the words were put to music, there were likely instrumental breaks or interludes. The purpose of the selah was probably to allow time to reflect on the meaning of what had just been sung. As the music played, people were to think about what they had just heard. So when we read the psalms and come to the word *selah,* it may be saying, "Pause and think about that."

What Sin Is All About

In Psalm 32 David is speaking about what God has done for him, how He had lifted a burden from him, and what a joy it is to be forgiven. In the Old Testament there are fifteen different words used to describe the word *sin*. In the first two verses of this psalm alone, David uses four of them: *transgression, sin, iniquity*, and *deceit*. Each has a different meaning, but when we put them together, we get a pretty good idea of what sin is all about.

Let's consider the first word—*transgression*. It reminds us that one characteristic of sin is defiance. *Transgression* connotes deliberately crossing the line or willfully sinning against God.

What happens when we place parameters on our children's behavior? We say, "Honey, don't do this. Don't do that. Don't touch the cookies. Don't cross the street." What's the first thing that some kids do after we issue a command like that? They put us to the test by going right to the edge. There's the cookie jar. Their tiny hands are a fraction of an inch away from it. Then they look at us to see what will happen if they cross the line. What's the penalty? If we enforce it, they will think twice before crossing that line again. If we let them get away with it, they conclude that commands mean nothing. A transgression involves deliberately crossing the line.

Sin is also a defect. Another word that David uses here for *sin* means "to miss the mark." It means there is something missing in our lives. We come up short of God's standards. Although humanity was originally created in the image of God, we became seriously flawed—damaged by sin that has infected the entire human race.

Iniquity is a third synonym for the word *sin*. It speaks of perverseness or crookedness. It reminds us that sin is a distortion or an aberration. God is saying that we are twisted and perverted inside. Another way to translate the word *iniquity* is that we are "bent, rather than straight." We are "crooked."

189

There's something askew in every person. While some of us are more bent than others, all of us have a flaw deep within.

Doletha Ward, a woman in Chicago, was driving along in her car and was apparently involved in a fender bender. The man in the other vehicle got out of his car, pulled Doletha out through the window of her car, chased her with a crowbar, struck her, and ripped her dress off. In desperation, the woman finally jumped into a nearby river, where she drowned. But this tragedy didn't happen on some isolated roadway. It all took place while cars drove by and a crowd of spectators cheered on the assailant.

People were shocked by this incident. It was the topic of national television news. The crime prompted revulsion and disbelief, but I'm sorry to say it doesn't surprise me. We are all twisted inside. We are all wicked to one degree or another. Sometimes we think we are so good—we are such a caring and compassionate community, and we are so cultured, civilized, and well mannered. The Bible says that the heart is deceitfully wicked. We would probably be shocked to know what we are actually capable of doing apart from God's restraining work and transformation in our lives.

Sin is also deceitful. We fool ourselves into believing that we can get away with sin, live with it, cover it up. But sin always finds us out. Why? Because we can't hide from God.

It is extremely rare to find people with hearts so tender that they will voluntarily confess their sins. In most cases confession only comes when people are confronted with their sins, as David was by Nathan. Even then, many people will refuse to confess unless provided with hard evidence of what wrong they have done.

Unfortunately, David had engaged in every form of sin that he mentions in Psalm 32. Clearly he had missed the mark. He had fallen short of the law's demands. He had also committed adultery and tried to cover it up with deceit. As a result, his life became crooked and twisted.

Sins of the Flesh, Sins of the Spirit

Not only did David commit sins of the flesh, he also committed sins of the spirit. What is the distinction? Second Corinthians 7:1 says, "Having these promises, beloved, let us cleanse ourselves from all filthiness of the flesh and spirit, perfecting holiness in the fear of God." What does that mean?

When David committed adultery and then murder, those were serious sins of the flesh, but when he covered up those sins, acted as though nothing had happened, and appeared to be righteous, he committed a sin of the spirit. By that I mean he willfully denied what he knew was true. David, after all, was not some pagan king who didn't understand that adultery and murder were wrong. He knew what he had done. He understood the law that God had given. Add to that the fact that David appeared to be a very spiritual person. Then, to add insult to injury, he had the audacity to want to condemn a man to death for killing a *sheep* when he had killed Bathsheba's husband. At the moment he appeared most spiritual, he was the most wicked. That was when he committed a sin of the spirit.

We can commit sins of the spirit without necessarily committing sins of the flesh. We know that people in our culture are committing sins of the flesh daily. They live as they please— hitting the bars, committing adultery, lying, stealing, and you name it. Christians often sit in judgment and recognize those sins as abominable, and they are. "Those people are sinners," we snort, "but I thank God I am so spiritual. Here I am in my Sunday best, driving to church with my wife and children. We're a wonderful family. Isn't that great?" But if we sit in church while living a double life, doing things that God has told us not to do, we are committing a sin of the spirit. Why? Because we know better. And a sin of the spirit is worse than a sin of the flesh. It's worse because knowledge brings responsibility.

That's why Jesus said to Pilate, the Roman governor, "The one who handed me over to you is guilty of a greater sin" (John 19:11, NIV). Who was it that handed Jesus over to Pilate? It was the high priest, Caiaphas. Why was the sin of Caiaphas greater than the sin of Pilate? Because Caiaphas, being the high priest, knew better. Caiaphas, being a man of God's Word, knew right from wrong. He sinned against the light. Whereas Pilate was just an ignorant, unbelieving pagan, Caiaphas willfully committed a sin of the spirit. Pilate sinned as well, but Caiaphas's sin was worse, Jesus said.

Psalm 32:3-4 describes the futility and misery of sin that is unconfessed. Look at the words the psalmist uses: "When I kept silent, my bones grew old through my groaning all the day long. . . . My vitality was turned into the drought of summer." It's miserable to live with unconfessed sin. Proverbs 28:13 says, "He who covers his sins will not prosper, but whoever confesses and forsakes them will have mercy." I have witnessed the truth of this passage many times in those who thought it somehow did not apply to them.

For instance, I have met people in church who seem to have their lives together. They claim that they want to walk with God and faithfully serve Him. They seem to do everything right—say the right things, have the right look, sound right. But something just isn't clicking. The Lord isn't blessing their lives or their endeavors. They go from one crisis to another saying, "Everyone is misrepresenting me. No one understands me."

We wonder, *What is wrong with these people?* Then one day it all comes out that they have been living in some sin that has not been confessed or renounced. It catches up with them as sin always does. Suddenly we realize why their lives have been such a mess and why things haven't been going well. The Bible explains it: "He who covers his sins will not prosper" (Proverbs 28:13).

No matter how we slice it, sin stinks. Its stench is going to permeate every area of our lives. We can't escape it. We can't put it in a safe little sin compartment and expect it to stay there. It just spreads, like a virus, through every area of our lives. It affects our marriage, our business, our free time, our spiritual life, and everything else. That's why it needs to be confessed and renounced.

Sin will even destroy our health if we don't deal with it. Not only is it bad for us spiritually, it's bad for us physically. This is obvious with people whose sin is the abuse of substances like alcohol or drugs. Even a star athlete like the late Mickey Mantle was not immune. Years of hard drinking resulted in the destruction of his liver. His sin was not only a spiritual issue, it also destroyed him physically. How many times have we seen this with celebrities in the entertainment world and in professional sports? It has become commonplace.

Stress and anxiety, the by-products of unconfessed sin, weigh heavily upon sinners, prematurely aging them. We see the evidence on their faces as worry eats them from the inside out. In fact, modern medical research has proven that worry and stress break down our resistance to disease. They attack the nervous system and can actually shorten human life.

Charles Mayo, founder of the famed Mayo Clinic, said he never knew anyone who died of overwork, but he knew many who died of worry. He said, "You can worry yourself to death, but you will never worry yourself into a longer life." Do you know anyone in that situation? Does that describe you right now? Are you gripped with worry because you are afraid your sin is going to come to the surface? That's how David felt. He said, "I groaned all day long. I was miserable."

Then in Psalm 32:5 he says, "I acknowledged my sin to

You, and my iniquity I have not hidden. I said, 'I will confess my transgressions to the Lord,' and You forgave the iniquity of my sin. Selah." Pause and think about that. This is the only way to deal with sin. We can't bury it and hope it will go away. It will come back again.

A little dog named Mugsy was hit by a car one day and was thought to be dead. The owners were heartbroken as they made the arrangements and had their precious little Mugsy buried in the local pet cemetery. The hardest part was knowing they would never see him again. Imagine their shock when, three days later, they heard something scratching on the screen door of their house, just the way Mugsy had. And there was a reason for that, for it was Mugsy, risen from the grave! Actually he didn't rise at all. He had never actually died and had been buried alive. Mugsy managed to dig himself out of his premature grave. It took him awhile, but he pawed his way to the surface and returned home.

That's a wonderful story, and it's a good illustration of sin. Just when we think we've buried our sin, just when it's out of sight and out of mind, it will come back. It will be at our back door before we know it, scratching at the screen, saying, "I'm still here. I'm not leaving you alone." But it will not be a happy sight. It will not be a cute little, long-lost pet. It will be our undoing.

There is only one place to get rid of sin—at the cross of Jesus Christ. We can't cover it. We can't hide it. We can't run from it. It will just stick to us until we confess it. David said, "I will confess my sin." Note his use of the word *my*. Over and over again, he personalizes the issue: My sin, my iniquity, my transgression. He admitted to God that it was he who had sinned. He didn't try to blame someone else or hide it at this point. He called it what it was and dealt with it in a straightforward way—the only way.

Blaming or Claiming Sin

Frederick the Great, king of Prussia, was visiting a prison on one occasion and talking with each of the inmates. As he listened to them, he heard endless tales of innocence, misunderstood motives, and exploitation. Apparently, no one in this prison was guilty. They were all framed. They all claimed innocence. The crimes were not their fault.

Finally the king stopped at the cell of a convict who remained silent. Frederick said, "Well, I suppose you, too, are an innocent victim?"

This man replied, "No sir, I'm not. I am guilty, and I deserve my punishment." Turning to the warden, the king shouted, "Quick, get this man out of here before he corrupts these other innocent people!" He couldn't believe he had found an honest man—someone who would own up to what he had done.

Do you need to own up to something you have done? Or are you playing the blame game? Blame never affirms; it always assaults. Blame never resolves; it always complicates. Blame never unites; it always separates. Blame never smiles; it always frowns. Blame never forgives; it always rejects. Blame never forgets; it always remembers. Blame never builds; it always destroys. *Selah*. Pause and think about that.

It's not my fault. It's his fault, her fault, anybody's fault but mine. There is going to come a time in life when we will have to admit, "We have sinned. We have committed iniquity. The problem is us." That's when things will change for us and change for the better.

What does it mean to confess our sins? Certainly that is important to know because our very forgiveness hinges on our understanding of the term. The Hebrew word translated *confess* means "to acknowledge." In the New Testament it could be translated "to agree with someone" or "to say the same thing as another." It's used in 1 John 1:9: "If we confess our sins, He is faithful and just to forgive us our sins and to cleanse us from all unrighteousness." The word *confess* essentially means that if you will agree with God about your sins, if you will acknowledge them and turn from them, you will be forgiven.

Here is the problem: People today often think they have confessed their sins when they haven't. Why? Because they think confession is merely acknowledgment. Therefore they sin, get caught, and say, "All right, you caught me. I confess that sin. It was a bad thing, and I won't do it again." Then they go out and do it again and again saying, "I did it again. I confess that sin." That's not confession. They are just acknowledging it, recognizing the obvious.

David didn't just acknowledge his past mistakes and his character flaws. He set out to change them with the help of God and the working of the Holy Spirit. Confession means to see our sins for what they really are, to be sorry for them, and to turn from them. We have to take our sins to the cross and recognize our offenses against our holy God. We must turn from our sins and stop making excuses for them. We have to be sorry enough to change. Then God will forgive us, and He will "cover."

The Great Cover-Up
David uses three important words in Psalm 32:2. He says, "Blessed is the man to whom the Lord does not impute iniquity." Before that, in verse 1, he says, "Blessed is he whose transgression is forgiven, whose sin is covered." This word *covered* means "concealed and out of sight." David had tried to cover his sins himself without success. But when God covers our sins, they are gone forever. We can't cover our sins, but God can. We can't get rid of them, but God can. Psalm 103:12 says, "As far as the east is from the west, so far has He removed our transgressions from us." God not only covers our sins, He cleanses them. There is no trace of them left.

Do you need to confess your sins? Do you need to turn from something in your life? Do you feel as David did— tormented inside, miserable, groaning all the day long? Do you need medication to help you get to sleep at night because your conscience isn't clear? God can change all of that. He can get to the root of your problems.

You can rediscover the spring in your step. You can say, as David did in the psalm, "Happy are those whose sins are forgiven." Do you long for that happiness? Or would you prefer to deceive yourself and others? The choice is yours.

We always have choices about our lives and the course they take. We can either confess our sins, turn from them, and know the happiness of being forgiven, or we can hide our sins, know the misery of being found out, and reap what we have sown.

Are your sins forgiven? Or are you reading this book without the hope or knowledge that your sins are forgiven—knowing that something in your life is not right with God, knowing that something is hindering your relationship with Him? If that's the case, you must know this: Until you deal with your sins, it's as if you have erected a wall between yourself and God.

The Bible says that if we conceal our sins or if we hold on to some sins, the Lord will not hear us. We may attempt to pray or draw close to the Lord, but the sins we have not dealt with must be confessed before we can find the forgiveness that God wants us to experience.

Some missionaries were trying to translate the Bible for some Eskimos in northern Alaska. They came upon the word *forgiven*, but they could find no word in the language of the Eskimos that corresponded to it. After much patient listening to the language of these people, they finally found a word that meant "not being able to even think about it anymore." That was the word they used for *forgiveness* in their Bible translation.

Not being able to even think about it anymore—that's a great concept. That's what forgiveness is. As God says in Jeremiah 31:34, "I will forgive their iniquity, and their sin I will remember no more."

If you have met the conditions for forgiveness of your sins, then they are forgiven and forgotten by God.

No one is exempt from the reach and tug of sin's allure. I think of a wonderful Christian couple, Bill and Christeen, who once attended the church I pastor. They had a powerful ministry traveling around, speaking to young people on high school campuses. God used them to bring many into His kingdom. I'm sure that is why the enemy set his sights on them, and in one of their lives he tragically succeeded.

I received this letter from Bill:

> As you know, Christeen and I are no longer husband and wife. Our marriage ended in divorce. Christeen remarried recently. Bottom line, Greg, I just took my eyes off of God and placed them on me and circumstances surrounding me. Pride, lust, and the enemy had their way. Before long, Christeen (God's gift to me) no longer satisfied me, and I committed adultery. In fact, the very night that act took place, you and I crossed paths at the mall. I was there at the restaurant sitting with a coworker, Cindy, whom I introduced to you, remember?

And I do remember. I walked by this little outdoor restaurant, where you can watch the people stroll by, and there sat Bill and a woman I didn't recognize. She certainly wasn't his wife.

When I first saw them, I didn't want to go to their table, thinking it might be uncomfortable for all. Then I reconsidered and decided to go right up to Bill. He seemed very uncomfortable, making me think this whole situation wasn't right. The woman he was with didn't seem concerned in the least. I asked Bill how Christeen was, and he told me all was well. But it was not. Reflecting now, I wish I had done and said more.

Bill continued:

> When I look back on that night, I think of when Judas came to Jesus in the Garden with the band of soldiers to arrest Jesus. Before Judas identified Christ with a kiss, Jesus said to him, "Friend, why have you come?" Jesus, in that moment of betrayal, was reaching out to Judas giving him one last chance.
>
> You were the person God used to cross my path that evening, to wake me up, to warn me, "Don't do this." I didn't listen. That decision and those to follow systematically destroyed my life.
>
> In 1995, I hit rock bottom. My life was in complete shambles. I had lost everything. My relationship with God, my marriage, and my reputation—everything was gone. Financially I was ruined. Gone. It was all gone.

How easily Bill's story could have stopped there. For many it does. Ironically, often when people reap the inevitable consequences of sin, they get angry with God! They blame Him for the sin they didn't resist.

Thankfully, Bill did not get bitter, he got better. He didn't turn from God but toward Him. To start with, he accepted full responsibility for his actions. He wrote:

> God is indeed a God of first, second, and third chances. I look back on my life and see the destruction that has been done because of selfishness. I failed to take God seriously at His word. I thought I knew what I was doing. "Step out of the way, God. You're crowding me!"

I virtually destroyed what life I had at that time. Even worse, I destroyed Christeen's life as well. Then there are Christeen's folks, aunts, uncles, grandparents, and the list goes on and on of the casualties that were produced because of a wrong decision followed by wrong actions.

Bill went to church and received some biblical counsel on what to do next. He got back in regular fellowship and Bible study and rearranged his priorities and focus in life. Finally, he wrote:

You know, Greg, all those years previous to my fall, I had known God's Word. I had ministered God's Word to quite a number of people as well. Looking back now, I'm able to see what I lacked, where I was weak enough to let this happen, and how to prevent this from happening again.

God has done a great work in my life thus far, and I'm looking forward to each new day, minute, and hour He gives me. In His grace He has extended me another opportunity to glorify Him through my life for that day. He has allowed me another opportunity to share Christ with another person or persons through the examples set forth in my words and deeds.

That is why with every new day, when that alarm clock sounds, the first words out of my mouth are those shared by the psalmist in Psalm 118:24: "This is the day the Lord has made; we will rejoice and be glad in it."

Yes, God graciously gave Bill a second chance. He can and will do the same for you. You can take that to the bank.

KEYS TO A LASTING FRIENDSHIP WITH GOD

*I no longer call you servants, because a servant does not
know his master's business. Instead, I have called you
friends, for everything that I learned from my Father I
have made known to you.*
    JOHN 15:15, NIV

Two friends decided to go on a camping trip together. One
morning as the two men were getting up for their morning
coffee, they looked up and saw a grizzly bear charging toward
them at full speed with a very hungry look on its face. One of
the men quickly grabbed his running shoes and started pulling
them on. His friend turned to him and said, "What are you
doing? Do you think you're going to outrun that grizzly bear?"

His friend replied, "I don't have to outrun the grizzly bear.
I just have to outrun you."

Sadly, that is how a lot of so-called friends behave. They
run out on us when times are hard. In fact, it's often a time of
hardship or crisis that determines who our real friends are. An
old adage says that a true friend walks in when others walk out.

The Greek philosopher Socrates had an even bleaker view
of friendship, saying, "Friends? There is no friend." Socrates'
problem was that he never knew the One who is described in
the Bible as "a friend who sticks closer than a brother" (Proverbs 18:24).

We have been looking at how we can find forgiveness for

our sins—how to have a second chance in our relationship with God. Now I want to shift gears and do a little preventive maintenance, believing that the best defense is a good offense. In other words, rather than solely concentrating on how to defend ourselves from temptation and the potential for sin, we should give more attention to cultivating a close and intimate walk with God. The more we know of Jesus and His great love for us, the more we will want to build that closeness and friendship with Him.

It's amazing to think that the Almighty God would actually offer us His friendship. Perhaps you've never looked at God as a friend. Maybe you've even entertained the thought that God somehow delights in seeing His creatures suffer or that He is just some remote, impersonal, unfeeling supreme being. Or you may see Him as some austere, harsh, demanding deity who means to make your life miserable. In reality, nothing could be further from the truth.

When God offers us His friendship, He is not asking to be one of our casual acquaintances who is there to check in on us periodically. Jesus Christ is extending His hand of friendship to us, and that is very significant. For you will never have a friend like this. Talk about having a friend in high places!

A Tangible Demonstration of Love

What proof do we have that God truly desires a close, personal friendship with us? He demonstrated His willingness to have friendship with us in a tangible way. During His ministry on earth, Jesus was referred to as "the friend of sinners." Interestingly, that statement was not originally intended as a compliment. But it certainly was the truth. Jesus was, and still is, the best friend sinners have ever had. He extends that hand of friendship to us right now, and if we will notice, that hand bears a wound in it—a wound He received when he went to the cross

to demonstrate His incredible love for us. He offered His friendship to us while we were still His enemies. That's why Jesus
says, "Greater love has no one than this, than to lay down one's
life for his friends" (John 15:13).

Let's think about it. Would we die for our husband or wife
or child? Many of us probably would. Would we die for a close
friend? Possibly. Would we die for a casual acquaintance?
Perhaps. Would we die for a coworker? I don't know; it
depends. But would we die for our worst enemy? I seriously
doubt it.

Imagine coming home from work, finding your house in
flames, then seeing a man jump out the front window of your
burning house with your new VCR in one hand and your laptop
computer in the other. Your anger is building when you see that
the man is headed straight into the path of a speeding truck.
You realize that if you run and push the man, you can save him,
but you will then fall into the path of this oncoming truck.
Would you do it? Probably not. More than likely you would like
to push him in the way of the truck while saving your laptop
computer and VCR. It's rare for someone to die for an enemy, if
not unheard of altogether.

Yet while we were still sinners—while we were the
enemies of God—He died for us, showing us the depth of His
friendship. All would want to enter into a relationship with this
God. Most anyone would like to honestly say, "God and me,
we're actually tight. He's actually a close friend of mine."

And we can, if we are Christians. For all practical
purposes, believers can legitimately make that claim. Yet some
of us fail to let our friendship with God go beyond a simple
introduction. As a result, we often become discouraged and
frustrated in our Christian walk. Our spiritual life lacks depth
and vitality. We are missing the joy that comes from experiencing true friendship with God.

How to Find Friendship with God

We cannot truly be the friend of a person with whom we have no interaction. Friendship is giving and taking. It involves offering something and then expecting the other party to reciprocate. If we really want to be true friends of God, certain requirements must be met. He is offering His friendship to us, but we must respond. Jesus lays out those requirements in John 15, which records one of His final talks with His disciples before His death.

1. *Friendship with God requires openness.* Jesus tells the disciples gathered around Him at that moment, "No longer do I call you servants, for a servant does not know what his master is doing; but I have called you friends, for all things that I heard from My Father I have made known to you" (John 15:15).

This verse powerfully illustrates the nature of the true friendship God desires with us. One thing stands out: A friend tells another friend his secrets. That's what distinguishes a mere acquaintance from a friend. Friends are the ones you call on the phone to tell what you are going through. When something wonderful happens in your life—you get a raise or a promotion, or that girl or guy says yes—could you imagine calling up a total stranger with the news? Open the phone book, pick a name at random, dial the number, and say, "Hi. You have never met me, but I want to share some good news with you." Of course not. You call a friend. "Guess what? Remember when I talked to you about this situation? Well, it happened!" And a true friend will rejoice with you. "That's great! I'm so happy for you."

Then again, a true friend is someone you can call when hardship hits. When you get that call from the doctor's office with bad news, when something falls through, when you are hurting, when you are struggling with some of the hard questions of life, a true friend will be there for you.

Jesus was saying, "I want to have a friendship with you." He was saying, "I am no longer calling you servants." That is significant, given the context of this chapter. John 15 begins the record of the last week in the life of our Lord before His crucifixion. In these final hours Jesus reveals things to His disciples that He could not have revealed to them before because they would have been unable to grasp them.

By then, however, as they had spent some time with Him and had matured and grown, Jesus could say, "I now want us to enter into a deeper relationship. Up to this point you have been my servants, and you still are. However, you are more than that, because a servant doesn't know what his master is doing, but now I'm letting you in on some inside information. I am revealing things to you now that I couldn't before. I'm telling you all the things My Father has told Me. I'm baring my heart to you."

That's exactly what He did. He spoke candidly about His crucifixion and the horrors He was going to face. Then a short time later He said to three of them—Peter, James, and John— "Would you three come with Me as I go over there to the garden? Would you just watch and pray, for the spirit is willing but the flesh is weak." Jesus was asking for some human companionship.

There in the Garden of Gethsemane, the Bible says that He cried out, "Father, if it is Your will, take this cup away from Me; nevertheless not My will, but Yours, be done" (Luke 22:42). And Scripture tells us that great beads of sweat dropped from His brow as if they were blood. He was going through a time of incredible anguish and difficulty as He contemplated the horrors and reality of the cross of Calvary. All He wanted His three friends to do was to be there for Him. Tragically, they decided to catch a little nap, and they slept through that opportunity. But we see Jesus baring His heart, opening Himself up. That's what a friend will do.

Maybe you have opened yourself up to some friends, but later they turned on you and betrayed you. That's certainly a hard thing to face. It often seems as if the ones you do the most for turn on you. An experience like that makes you a little apprehensive about having friends. You wonder to yourself, *Can anyone really be trusted?* Although I can't assure you that all of your friends will always stand by you through thick and thin, I can assure you that God, who wants to be your friend, will always keep your confidence. You can reveal your heart to Him, reveal your secrets to Him, share anything with Him. He understands you, loves you, cares about you, and He will always be there for you.

2. *Friendship with God requires truthfulness.* Real friends tell the truth to each other. When we know someone well, we are honest, candid. We don't necessarily screen all our statements before we make them. We know that they know us and understand that we may blow off a little steam every now and then. If they say or do something we don't necessarily agree with, we tell them.

This isn't the case with people who are not emotionally close. Maybe you're going out with someone you don't really know all that well, and she says, "Hey, I just got this new outfit. What do you think?" You don't really like the outfit, but not feeling comfortable enough with her to be blunt, you say, "It looks great. Let's go." A true friend, when asked the same question, may say, "You're not actually going out wearing that, are you?" Friends know they can always get honest answers from each other. The Bible says, "Faithful are the wounds of a friend, but the kisses of an enemy are deceitful" (Proverbs 27:6). Enemies will flatter us. They will tell us that we are great and that everything is wonderful. Then, behind our back, they will cut us down. In contrast, true friends will tell us the truth to our face. As author Oscar Wilde said, "A true friend always stabs you in the front."

In John 15 and 16 Jesus doesn't hide anything from His

disciples. He explains the cost of being a true friend, but He also gives them reason to hope. Jesus tells His disciples what to expect in the future. He doesn't try to conceal the truth or lie about the facts. He is honest with us, and we should be nothing less with Him.

Even though God is omniscient, knowing everything about us, He still desires our honesty. When Adam and Eve sinned in the Garden of Eden, God didn't come straight out and say, "Adam, you blew it!" Instead, He sought him out, asking, "What is this you have done?" (Genesis 3:13). God wants us to confess our sins to Him. He wants us to share our heart's desire with Him. He wants to hear about our troubles.

When we have an open and honest friendship with God, our spiritual life will move forward. The psalmist David understood this, and he penned the following words: "Search me, O God, and know my heart; test me and know my anxious thoughts. See if there is any offensive way in me, and lead me in the way everlasting" (Psalm 139:23-24, NIV).

Jesus should be our example when it comes to being a friend and making friends. We should be able to look at our friends and say, "Because I love you, because I care about you, I have to share this with you. I think you are making a mistake. I don't think you should do thus and so." Since we care about them, we will tell them the truth.

The same principle should apply in our personal choice of friends. That's why we want to look for godly companions in life. We cannot necessarily control our environment at all times—our neighbors, our coworkers, people we meet during the day. But we can decide who our close friends will be. We must give serious consideration to those people with whom we spend our free time and bare our heart. It's important to look for others who love God and who encourage us spiritually. The Scriptures say, "Do not be misled: 'Bad company corrupts good character' " (1 Corinthians 15:33, NIV). We will be influenced by our friends, and they will be influenced by us. The Bible also says, "Flee the evil desires of youth, and pursue righteousness, faith, love and peace, along with those who call on the Lord out of a pure heart" (2 Timothy 2:22, NIV). We must look for friends who are passionate in their commitment to Jesus Christ—people who will encourage us in that pursuit.

If you are presently engaged in a friendship—or even worse, a romantic entanglement—with someone who is dragging you down spiritually or always trying to get you to compromise, sever that relationship. Don't stay in a relationship that could be detrimental to your walk with God. Instead, look for people who will help you move forward in your walk with God.

3. *Friendship with God requires obedience to Him.* How do we show our love toward God? How do we demonstrate our friendship with Him? The answer is found in John 15:14, where Jesus says, "You are My friends if you do whatever I command you." The way we demonstrate our friendship with Jesus is to do what He says. If we don't, we really have no right to call ourselves His friends.

Many of us do not obey Jesus. We intentionally break His commandments over and over again. Then we periodically go to God and say, "I'm sorry. I have done this horrible thing. But I'll make up for it. I'll go to another church service this week. I'll sing a little louder in the worship service, and I'll give a large financial gift to the church."

God would answer us, "I don't want your large financial gifts. I don't want you to sing louder. I just want you to obey Me. If you don't obey Me, those other things don't make up for it. In fact, those other things can even be offensive to Me." He told Israel, "Away with the noise of your songs! I will not listen to the music of your harps" (Amos 5:23, NIV). Does that mean God doesn't appreciate heartfelt worship? No, but it does mean that if we're going to disobey Him continually, our praise is not sincere. In fact, it's distasteful to Him. First and foremost, God wants our obedience.

King Saul was ultimately rejected by the Lord to rule Israel because of his constant wickedness and disobedience. In 1 Samuel 15 the Lord instructed Saul to go into battle against his enemies and destroy them completely, along with their livestock. But as he was defeating the enemy on the battlefield, Saul saw some choice sheep and cattle, and he decided to keep them for himself. So he gave his men the order "Take those back to my home." And they did.

The next day the prophet Samuel met King Saul. Saul greeted the prophet and said, "Samuel, good to see you. Bless you in the name of the Lord!"

Samuel replied, "I have a question for you, Saul. Did you do all that the Lord commanded you?"

"Yes, I did everything. I destroyed the enemies of the Lord. I did just as the Lord told me to."

"Then why is it I hear the bleating of the sheep and the lowing of the cattle in the background?" Samuel asked.

"Thanks for bringing that to my attention," Saul said with a satisfied smile. "I saved the best of the sheep and cattle to sacrifice to the Lord. I was just getting ready to mention that to you."

I love Samuel's response: "Does the Lord delight in burnt offerings and sacrifices as much as in obeying the voice of the Lord? To obey is better than sacrifice, and to heed is better than the fat of rams" (1 Samuel 15:22, NIV). Samuel was saying, "First and foremost, God wants your obedience. Your worship, your praise, your giving, your service—all those things are fine in their place. But obedience must come first."

Jesus said, "If you love Me, obey Me."

4. *Friendship with God requires active obedience.* Jesus said, "You are My friends if you do whatever I command you" (John

15:14). Some people think it's enough if they avoid what God forbids. They say, "I am a Christian, and as a Christian I don't do certain things anymore. I've made many changes in my life—I'm not a thief, I'm not an adulterer, I don't murder." That's like saying, "I'm your friend because I don't rob you, cheat you, insult you, or beat you up." Now while I appreciate the fact that my friend doesn't rob, cheat, insult or beat me up, friendship is more than that—and the same should be true of our friendship with God.

Being a Christian is not just keeping a list of rules and regulations or merely avoiding wrong. It is also doing right. It's not merely the avoidance of evil; it's embracing what is right. Psalm 1:1 says, "Blessed is the man who walks not in the counsel of the ungodly, nor stands in the path of sinners, nor sits in the seat of the scornful." True, this person doesn't do certain things that could hinder his relationship with God, but he also takes some positive action. The passage goes on to say, "But his delight is in the law of the Lord, and in His law he meditates day and night (v. 2)." That's what I call "active obedience."

Is your delight in the law of the Lord? Are you finding joy in your friendship and relationship with God? When you are satisfied in your relationship with God and doing the things that please Him, many of those things that used to attract you will become less appealing. Your desire instead will be to please God.

5. *Friendship with God requires continual obedience.* In the original language of the text, when Jesus says, "You are my friends if you do whatever I command you," it connotes a continuous process. It's not just something we do once in a while. It's a constant, repeated obedience. That doesn't mean we have to be perfect, because we are going to fail at times. But when we fail, we need to repent, get up, and try again. Although we have made that commitment to the Lord, we need to reaffirm that commitment every day.

In 1974 I stood before a group of people and pledged my love to my wife, Cathe, and she pledged hers to me. We said we would be faithful to each other, honor each other, and love each other until death parts us. By the grace of God, I have kept my vows to her, and she has kept hers to me. And I plan, with God's help, to continue to keep that commitment. Although I made that vow to her years ago, I reaffirm that commitment on a daily basis by honoring it. It's not enough to say that I obeyed God twenty years ago or fifteen years ago or one year ago. Every day I reaffirm that commitment of obedience to Him through my actions.

6. *Friendship with God requires obedience in even the smallest matters.* Jesus said, "You are My friends if you do whatever I command you." He didn't say, "You are My friends if you do whatever you are personally comfortable with." Nor did He say, "You are My friends if you do whatever you personally agree with," or, "You are My friends if you do whatever you find easy." He said, "You are My friends if you do whatever I command you."

This means we must obey God in every area. If the Bible tells us to stay away from a certain thing, even if we don't think it's significant, it means we obey the Word of God because we know our friend God is looking out for us. If He says, "Greg, don't do this," that means it will hurt me. And if He says, "Greg, you should do this," it means it will help me. I need to learn to trust my friend. It's not for me to second-guess God or try to edit His Word.

You might be thinking, *This is kind of nitpicky. I don't think I have to obey this. The big things, like the Ten Commandments, I can understand. But these little things—I just don't think they are necessary.* Jesus said, "You are My friends if you do whatever I command you."

7. *Friendship with God requires a willing obedience.* True friends of Jesus obey Him because they want to. They desire to please Him with their lives.

When we are in love, we naturally want to do the things that would please the ones we love. When I shop for something for my wife at Christmas, I don't do it out of obligation. I don't think, *Oh man, I have to get something for her again? Didn't I do that last year? And for her birthday and our anniversary—what a drag!* I don't feel that way. I enjoy it. I like to shop for Cathe, just as I like to do things for my children and my friends. I don't buy a gift for Cathe because I'm afraid of what she will do to me if I don't get her something. It's not done out of fear but out of love.

Likewise, we should obey Jesus because we love Him. We should not obey out of fear, worrying that if we fail to obey Him, God will do something horrible to us. When we really love the Lord, it's our delight, our joy, and our privilege to do what He commands. As Paul said, "The love of Christ compels us" (2 Corinthians 5:14).

Yes, God can be a friend to all of us. We can trust Him. People are going to let us down, but we have a friend who will never betray our confidence. We have a friend to whom we can tell our secrets and who will declare His secrets to us. We have the ultimate friend in high places—Jesus Christ. He wants to be our God. He wants to be our Savior and Lord and Master. But He also wants to be our friend.

What If I Don't Want to Be That Close to God?

Maybe you've become a bit uncomfortable with this chapter. You don't really know if you want to be in such an intimate relationship with your Creator. You may be like the little girl who, when told by her mother that she could not play with her friends until she got over her cold, said, "I wish I didn't have any parents." When asked why, she replied with a grin, "Because then I wouldn't have to listen to them!" The little girl didn't want to have the accountability that is required in the parent/child relationship. She failed to see that her parents had her best interest in mind. Likewise, some people are afraid of the responsibility that a friendship with God requires. They don't want to have to listen to Him, much less obey Him. They would rather have a casual acquaintance without any strings attached.

If you feel this way, I have sad news for you. If you are not the friend of God, you are His enemy. You may respond, "What do you mean His enemy? I'm not His enemy; I'm just not His friend. I don't want to be His anything. I just don't want to get involved." You are like Pontius Pilate, who, when facing the option of freeing Jesus or ordering His death, said, "I wash my hands of this matter." But once you have heard the statements of Jesus, you cannot wash your hands of the matter. You are His friend, or you are His enemy. The Bible says that if you love this world system, you are the enemy of God. Jesus Himself said, "He who is not with Me is against Me" (Matthew 12:30).

Now that you have seen the definition of what a friend of God really is, could you be called one? Does your relationship with Him go beyond just some mushy emotional feeling to display an obedience that is given willfully and continuously in all matters? If not, surrender your heart completely to God, and begin to actively seek Him and obey Him. It will be a friendship like no other you have ever known.

THE FREEDOM OF FORGIVENESS

The Lord gives freedom to the prisoners.
    PSALM 146:7

Sin holds us captive like magnificent tropical birds in a rusted cage. God's creatures are meant to fly free in His divine glory, but sin clips our wings and relegates us to pecking around for meager seed on a newspaper floor. Sin—unforgiven sin—preys on us as a hungry cat does a pretty bird. If we don't take flight, we will be devoured. Flight is our only hope of escape.

Freedom comes with forgiveness—a freedom like no other: freedom from worry, freedom from fear, freedom from the control of evil. Forgiveness opens the cage door and lets us mount up with wings like eagles into the glory of God. It preens our feathers, heals our wings, and renews our song. Forgiveness is God's eternal gift; all we have to do is accept it.

The freedom of forgiveness comes to us in two ways: knowing we can get it and knowing we already have it. Knowing we can get it comes with knowing God's promise: "If we confess our sins, he is faithful and just and will forgive us our sins and purify us from all unrighteousness" (1 John 1:9, NIV). That's a promise! "If we walk in the light, as he is in the light, we have fellowship with one another, and the blood of Jesus, his Son, purifies us from all sin" (1 John 1:7, NIV). *Have* and *purifies* are both in the present tense. We already have forgiveness, and He continually purifies us from all our sins.

We have explored God's promises, and we know how to get forgiveness by sincerely repenting. How, though, do we "walk in the light" so that we can know we are in fellowship with God and have constant forgiveness? How can we live in the freedom of forgiveness?

Back to Basics

Have you ever been embarrassed to find out you didn't really know as much as you thought you did? Recently I received one of those notices in the mail that we all come to dread. It was time for me to go down and take my written driving test again. Maybe one of the reasons I don't like to take driving tests is that I never did well on tests in school. I always had a hard time with them.

I thought to myself, *I have been driving for more than twenty-five years. I don't think that I need to read their manual again. I think by now I know the rules of the road.* So I casually strolled down to the Department of Motor Vehicles for my appointment. A person handed the little driving test to me and sent me over to a corner. As I took the test, I must admit some of the questions stumped me a bit, but I thought I did reasonably well. I knew I could miss only three and still pass.

I then took the completed test to the lady designated as the test checker. I watched her as she pulled out her red pen and with great relish began to go through my test. She marked one wrong. *Only two to go*, I thought. She marked another. *I can only get one more wrong!* I began to panic. Still most of the questions were left. Then three check marks . . . four, five, six.

"You have to take the test again," she said dryly, without a hint of sympathy.

I said, "I have a question. How many times can I take the test in one day?"

She said, "You can take it three times, but if you fail it the third time, not only will you have to come again and take the written test, but you will have to take a driving test as well."

I suddenly felt like I was sixteen again. Remembering I had failed my original driving test twice when I was that age, I was not looking forward to repeating that miserable experience. I passed the written test, barely. Actually, technically I failed. I pointed out to the person correcting the test that one of the things she said I had answered incorrectly was actually correct. She gave that to me. I walked out of there with my picture taken and my license coming in the mail. Thank God! But it was a humiliating experience. It reminded me that I don't necessarily know as much as I think I do. Even though I drive every single day and think I know all of the basics of driving, I obviously don't. Isn't it a surprise to find out we don't know as much as we think?

Of course, there are also those things that we learned but have simply forgotten. Maybe we could recite something from memory or always think of people's names. Then one day we forget an important phone number, or we run into an acquaintance at the store and completely forget his name! We do forget things in life—things that we think we know but we really don't know as well as we ought.

A group of students recently discovered this firsthand. What follows is a sampling of some of the strange answers teachers came across as they graded their students' Bible exams:

One student wrote, "In the first book of the Bible, the book of Genesis, Adam and Eve were created from an apple tree." That's an interesting twist.

Another said, "God asked Abraham to offer Isaac on Mt. Montezuma."

Regarding the story of Jacob and Esau, one student remarked, "Jacob stole his brother's birthmark." Now that would be difficult to do!

According to one other student, Pharaoh forced the Hebrew slaves to make bread (instead of bricks) without straw.

Another said, "Moses led the Israelites to the Red Sea, where they made unleavened bread, which is made without any ingredients." At least it would be fat-free.

One student, detailing the leadership of Moses, said, "Afterward Moses went up to Mt. Cyanide to get the Ten Commandments." Sounds like a one-way trip to me.

Still another said, "David was a Hebrew king skilled at playing the liar." The student didn't mean it that way, of course, but it does have a ring of truth to it, unfortunately.

Finally, my favorite: "Solomon, one of David's sons, had five hundred wives and five hundred porcupines." A very prickly situation!

We may laugh at answers this absurd. I'm sure you personally know the Bible much better than that. But I recently read of a survey that pointed out that those who read the Bible on a regular basis are often uncertain about its features. For instance, half of them could not name any of the four Gospels in the New Testament. The other half could name only one. Fewer than half who said they read the Bible on a regular basis knew who delivered the Sermon on the Mount. But the statistic that really amazed me was that of the 60 percent of Americans who attended church last Easter, only one-fourth of them knew what the holiday was about. That means that three-fourths of the 60 percent didn't even know what Easter was commemorating!

We don't really know as much as we think we know. Why? Part of the reason could be that we need to be reminded of certain things. We can easily lose sight of some of the basic truths and principles of God's Word. And when that happens, the results can be disastrous.

218

Reminders for the Believer

If we want to stand firm in our walk with the Lord and know His constant forgiveness, if we have stumbled in the past and want to keep from stumbling again, we need to frequently review even those basic things we think we already know. That is one of the reasons Peter wrote his second epistle: "For this reason I will not be negligent to remind you always of these things, though you know and are established in the present truth. Yes, I think it is right, as long as I am in this tent, to stir you up by reminding you, knowing that shortly I must put off my tent, just as our Lord Jesus Christ showed me" (2 Peter 1:12-14). Obviously, Peter was drawing upon what had been previously said: "I want you to remember these things that I have just said to you."

In the preceding verses, Peter lists a number of things God has placed in His Word that we should always keep at the forefront of our minds as Christians:

His divine power has given to us all things that pertain to life and godliness, through the knowledge of Him who called us by glory and virtue, by which have been given to us exceedingly great and precious promises, that through these you may be partakers of the divine nature, having escaped the corruption that is in the world through lust.

But also for this very reason, giving all diligence, add to your faith virtue, to virtue knowledge, to knowledge self-control, to self-control perseverance, to perseverance godliness, to godliness brotherly kindness, and to brotherly kindness love. For if these things are yours and abound, you will be neither barren nor unfruitful in the knowledge of our Lord Jesus Christ. For he who lacks these things is shortsighted, even to blindness, and has forgotten that he was cleansed from his old sins.

Therefore, brethren, be even more diligent to make

your call and election sure, for if you do these things you will never stumble; for so an entrance will be supplied to you abundantly into the everlasting kingdom of our Lord and Savior Jesus Christ. (2 Peter 1:3-11)

The Keys to Freedom

Notice that Peter says, "If you do these things, you will never stumble." That is significant considering that these words are coming from a man who knew a little bit about stumbling and falling. He himself had forsaken his own Lord, so you might say that he was something of an expert on the subject.

The words take on even greater significance when you bear in mind that they are some of the final words given by Simon Peter in his last epistle. Here was a man who had personally walked with Jesus during His earthly ministry and continued to walk with Him many years afterward. He had learned many of life's lessons the hard way. He was no longer the self-centered, impulsive disciple he had once been. He was a changed man. Now he was saying, "Here is what I have learned over the years as I have walked with Jesus Christ. Here are the basic truths that I have always tried to keep at the forefront of my mind. They are truths that must never be forgotten, truths that must always be focused on, truths that bring freedom. Failure to do these things will spell spiritual disaster."

Not only does Peter give us these truths, but he attaches two promises to them. First, he says that if we do these things, we will never stumble or fall. That's a great promise. Second, he says that we will have an abundant entrance into the kingdom of God. So if we don't want to stumble or fall, and if we want to have an abundant entrance into the kingdom of God, we must apply the truths that we have just read.

So what truths must we remember? What is it that we should be striving for? What does God require of us?

The Goal: To Become More like God[1]

God wants us to become more like Him, and the more we know God, the more we will understand that process. This is the basic definition the New Testament gives in describing the character, quality, and nature of the Christian life. What is it that I should desire as a Christian above everything else? Is it to have certain experiences? No. It is to know God and become more like Him. In fact, Jesus, speaking to God in John 17:3, says, "This is eternal life, that they may know You, the only true God, and Jesus Christ whom You have sent."

Many people start there, saying, "I believe that I know God. I made that commitment at an evangelistic crusade. I walked forward at the pastor's invitation to follow Jesus Christ on a Sunday and gave my life to Christ. I believe that I am now a child of God." That's great, but there is more to it than just meeting Him, more than just being introduced to Him. Now comes the quest, the purpose, the goal of the Christian life, the outgrowth of this friendship with God. Now we must become more like Him. He wants us to become "partakers of the divine nature" (2 Peter 1:4).

Every day we should be seeking to become more like Jesus Christ. Christians are the ones in whom we find the traits and characteristics of God Himself—not just those who believe that their sins are forgiven, but those who partake of the divine nature. I am, as a Christian, to be a new person and to manifest these characteristics. I don't mean that we are going to become gods. That certainly will never happen. Nor do I mean that we are even going to reach some state of perfection. What I am saying—and, more significantly, what the Bible is saying—is that I am to become more like God every day. That should be my goal.

You may say, "Greg, who can measure up to these things? Who can be like this? We all fall short." That's true, so what should we do—just give up and not even try? Should we tell ourselves that it can't be done? No, if God tells you to do something, it can be done. You're not going to reach perfection until you get to heaven, but you can become more like God and more Christlike over the years.

The Provision: God's Unlimited Power and Resources

How do we reach the goal of becoming more Christlike? The answer is found in 2 Peter 1:3: "His divine power has given to us all things that pertain to life and godliness, through the knowledge of Him who called us by glory and virtue." If God says you can do it, you can do it. The calling of God is the enabling of God. These words are not written to a group of spiritual elitists. They aren't directed to a special little holy club out there somewhere. They are to all people who call themselves followers of Christ.

Everything we need is given to us in God's Word. He has put everything there for our use. We cannot add to it. It doesn't say He has given to us *some* things that pertain unto life and godliness. It's not Jesus Christ plus emotional experience. It's not Jesus Christ plus psychology. It's not Jesus Christ plus this or that. It's Jesus Christ and Jesus Christ alone. Everything we need to live a godly life is found in Jesus Christ and is taught to us through His Word. We need go no further. We don't need to find some self-proclaimed prophet to tell us his latest revelation (for a fee, of course). We need to apply the Word of God and realize that God's Word and power are sufficient. When we fail to see that, we sell God short.

The Obstacle: This World

Not only does Peter tell us what the goal is and where the power comes from, but he also tells us what the problem is. It's good to know what obstacles are in our paths. In verse 4, Peter says that we have "escaped the corruption that is in the world through lust." This world will not support us in our quest to know God. In fact, it will try to pull us down. We must see this world for what it is and ourselves for what we are by nature.

Because of the Fall and the sin that is inherited by every man and woman, we realize that we live in a world system that is hostile to God. By biblical definition, the world system is "all that is in the world—the lust of the flesh, the lust of the eyes, and the pride of life" (1 John 2:16). That verse goes on to say such things are not of the Father but are "of the world." Basically, when the Bible speaks of the world, it is referring to the thinking, the mentality, the way of living that people choose apart from Jesus Christ. The reasoning of the world says, "I must look out for myself. I am all that matters. The whole world revolves around me." We can never know God or become more like Him until we see ourselves as we really are and until we see this world as it really is. The moment we recognize that, we have taken the first step to becoming more godly people.

A Diligent Quest

In verse 5 of this passage Peter says, "For this very reason, giving all diligence . . ." Another way to translate that phrase would be, "Because of this, give all diligence." In other words, because I realize that God wants me to know Him and become like Him, because I realize that the world is opposing me and will stop me from this quest, I must give all diligence to these matters.

Peter lists the attributes that we should diligently seek in a specific order, but he doesn't ask us to do anything for God until he highlights what God has done for us. The Bible's emphasis is always on what God has done for us. Everything that we are called to do is in *response* to God's initiative. As we grow in our appreciation of all that the Lord has done for us, we naturally will want to reciprocate. We will want to show our gratitude.

We will want to show our thankfulness for receiving His unmerited favor.

God has given us everything we need as Christians to live lives that are full and purposeful and, most important, pleasing to Him. Our accounts are not empty, but full. We have more than we can ever use. We have unlimited resources.

Check the account. Here is what it says: "His divine power has given to us all things that pertain to life and godliness, through the knowledge of Him who called us by glory and virtue" (2 Peter 1:3). The Bible also says that "God is able to make all grace abound toward you, that you, always having all sufficiency in all things, may have an abundance for every good work" (2 Corinthians 9:8). That's God's word to you. *All* that you need for life and godliness has been provided. It's more than sufficient. He has given to you these great promises. That's what God has done for you.

Give Your All in This Quest

In recognition of what God has done, Peter describes what we are supposed to do. "But also for this very reason, giving all diligence, add to your faith virtue, to virtue knowledge, to knowledge self-control, to self-control perseverance, to perseverance godliness, to godliness brotherly kindness, and to brotherly kindness love" (2 Peter 1:5-7).

The word *diligence* in this passage could be translated "with intense effort." Have you ever watched someone do something in a halfhearted manner? If you have kids, I'm sure you will probably say yes. When you give them a chore to do, many will do it, but few will give it their all.

One may say, "I've already cleaned my room."

Then you walk him to his room and say, "Try for a moment to see this through my eyes. Do you see that large heap of clothing? Well, underneath that somewhere is something called your bed that has not been made in a long time. This is not what I would call clean."

Sadly, some people undertake the Christian life the same way. They pray halfheartedly, read the Bible halfheartedly, worship and give halfheartedly, share their faith halfheartedly. They do everything in a half-baked way.

God gave His best to you. He deserves nothing less than your best in return. Be diligent. Apply yourself with intense effort to what God says.

Add Virtue

Peter tells us to add virtue to our faith. God has given faith to every one of us as Christians. What we do with it is up to us. Faith is a lot like a muscle—it grows with use.

At the beginning of a new year many of us start to feel guilty about the extra food we ate over the holidays. So we resolve to join a health club and start exercising regularly. We put on our brand-new workout outfit we got for Christmas. We pump the iron. We climb on the stair machine. And we feel so good about ourselves. But the next day we suddenly feel the pain. Everything hurts. As a result, a lot of us stop. Others pursue it. They continue to work out. It still hurts, but their muscles begin to grow. They develop more stamina and get stronger by the day.

Faith is much the same way—it grows through use. Still, a number of us treat our faith as though it were some kind of museum piece. Someone comes over to visit and we say, "Do you want to see my faith? Come over here. I have it encased in glass. Look at it, but don't breathe on it."

The faith of many Christians reminds me of the people who buy 4x4 vehicles. It's a popular trend right now—everybody is driving trucks. Some guys have "tricked-out" rigs. They have everything on them—massive off-road tires, huge roll bars with the extra lights on top, the whole winch apparatus on the front, and the towing hardware on the back. These guys are ready for action, but where do we see them? Usually at the car wash.

"Just get back from four-wheeling?" you may ask a proud owner.

"No, I just drove down the street."

"Where are you off to?" you ask.

"I'll probably go to another car wash. It will get dirty on the way over," he replies.

"Why don't you go four-wheeling?"

"What, are you nuts?! Do you realize how much money I have in this thing?" he exclaims.

They don't use that rugged all-terrain vehicle for what it was intended. Likewise, many Christians don't take the faith that God has given them and do anything with it. It just lies dormant. But faith is not meant to be static or to lie dormant. Instead, we are supposed to add virtue to our faith lavishly— diligently—"with intense effort."

We hear a lot about virtue nowadays. One of the most popular books written in recent years is William Bennett's *The Book of Virtues*. One of the reasons for its popularity is that we have lost sight of what virtue is in our society. We are confused about what is right and wrong. We have lost so many virtues that are important for the preservation of our culture.

The Greek word Peter uses for *virtue* means "moral power or energy." The power to live morally comes from what we are spiritually. That is why any debate on the subject of morality that leaves out spirituality is a failure. For how are we to decide what is moral? Without God's values, whose values will we follow? We have wrongly redefined morality into whatever suits us or whatever is convenient. That's what is wrong with this world's definition. So when we say we need to develop values in our country, we need to go back to what the Bible says.

Some people will say, "But that's religion. We can't have religion in this." I'm sorry, but you cannot have morality without religion. And, more significant, you cannot have true virtue without Jesus Christ. He is the key.

Add Knowledge

Peter says we should add knowledge to virtue. We can have moral energy, but it needs to be tied to knowledge; otherwise we just have a lot of energy we don't know how to direct.

Some churches emphasize experiencing God. The whole worship service is built around emotion and excitement—an experience. So the whole focus is, "God, touch us. We need that feeling, that touch from You." But so often people who attend such a service go away disappointed because God may not have done what they expected Him to do.

Other churches build everything around correct teaching, "rightly dividing the word of truth" (2 Timothy 2:15). Everything is accurate, and that's important, but I suggest that we need to see both ends of the spectrum. We need the Word accurately presented, rightly divided, and properly taught, but we also need virtue, energy, excitement, and passion as we put His Word into practice.

That's what Peter is saying here: We need moral energy, virtue. But we need to temper it with knowledge. You could call it "knowledgeable virtue." It's not just a display of energy without control.

Add Self-Control

Then Peter turns to inner qualities. First, he says, we need self-control. We all need self-control in general, but Peter is speaking here of self-control in a specific area of life. When Peter says we need self-control, he is speaking of sexual passion. It seems that we need this more than ever today. We have seen so many lives devastated by immorality. Peter says we need to control ourselves. We can do it, because God has given us the power to do it. This isn't something we don't have any say over. After all, James 1:14 says, "Each one is tempted when he is drawn away by his own desires and enticed." It's a choice we make. We can decide what we'll use to fill our mind, with whom we will spend our time, and to what we will yield.

This idea is summed up well in Romans 6:12-13: "Do not let sin reign in your mortal body so that you obey its evil desires. Do not offer the parts of your body to sin, as instruments of wickedness, but rather offer yourselves to God, as those who have been brought from death to life; and offer the parts of your body to him as instruments of righteousness" (NIV). So instead of yielding to wrong, yield to right.

This is why we will not stumble or fall if we do these things. We will be so actively engaged in the pursuit of God that we will not have the time and energy to pursue what is evil. I'm not saying we are somehow going to be temptation proof, for there is no such thing. I'm not saying we will never sin again. But I am saying we will be so enamored of God, so impassioned with serving and following Him and becoming more like Him, that the things of this world will simply not have the appeal they once had.

Add Endurance

While we need self-control, we also need perseverance, or endurance. Peter knew about this, too. He is the disciple who denied His Lord three times. There is little point in making great professions if we don't carry them out. We need to cultivate patient endurance, not some roller-coaster "Jesus is everything to me" outlook one day and "God who?" the next. We need to be consistent in our faith, remembering the resources He has given us and the objectives He has set before us.

Add Godliness

Peter speaks of seeking to be like God in all we say and do. Scripture tells us, "Let this mind be in you which was also in Christ Jesus" (Philippians 2:5). That's a tall order. How do we do it? "Let nothing be done through selfish ambition or conceit, but in lowliness of mind let each esteem others better than himself. Let each of you look out not only for his own interests, but also for the interests of others" (Philippians 2:3-4). Being a godly person, among other things, is to think of the needs of others and be compassionate and concerned about them.

Charles H. Spurgeon once said, "Of what value is the grace I profess to receive if it does not dramatically change the way that I live? If it doesn't change the way that I live, it will never change my eternal destiny."

Add Brotherly Kindness

To godliness, we must add brotherly kindness. How important this is. It stems first from our relationship to God. The more godly and Christlike we become, the more we begin to see people as Jesus sees them.

I don't know when our culture has ever been more divided. It seems that in our attempt to celebrate our diversity and individualism, we are becoming more separated from one another. We are divided along racial lines, separated along economic lines, and split along gender lines. Unfortunately, we often carry this baggage with us into church, where the barriers must be removed. We should not see others as this or that but as brothers or sisters in Jesus Christ, whom we love unconditionally. We are the family of God, and that's the tightest bond of all. We are commanded to love one another.

A Call to Refocus

To fail to have these qualities, to fail to desire these qualities, should be a warning sign: "He who lacks these things is short-sighted, even to blindness, and has forgotten that he was cleansed from his old sins" (2 Peter 1:9). The word for *blindness* could also be translated "to deliberately close your eyes." If you don't have these qualities, you are deliberately closing your eyes to what is important. The person who claims to be a Christian but yet is not seeking to know God and become more like Him is missing the boat. Christians who are not concerned with moving forward in life are in serious trouble. They are not looking at the big picture. They are not looking at the spiritual but only at the temporal.

We need to look beyond the present moment. We need to refocus on our promised reward as Peter did: If you do these things, "an entrance will be supplied to you abundantly into the everlasting kingdom of our Lord and Savior Jesus Christ" (2 Peter 1:11).

Tradition tells us that Peter was crucified upside down. We don't know if this is true, but it is a strong possibility. According to tradition, the reason Peter was crucified upside down is because when they were going to crucify him right side up, he said, "I am not worthy to die in the same manner as my Lord did."

Peter knew death was coming. So he said, "Here is what is really important to me. Here is what I have learned over the years. I am going to have an entrance supplied to me. You can have it supplied to you. I am looking forward to that day." He died without any regrets because he lived without any regrets. He was ready to die as he had lived—serving and following Jesus. He was ready to face the One who died for him and hear the words, "Well done, good and faithful servant." He had made the most of his second chance.

I ask you right now, as you look back on your life, have you been seeking to know God and become more like Him?

Have you been focused on a life that honors God? Or have you been living merely for yourself—living for the moment?

In closing, my great hope is that this book will have persuaded you that there is a second chance for everyone who sincerely asks for it and accepts it. If you focus on these things you should never forget, God says you will never stumble or fall. And He will give you an abundant entrance into His kingdom. If you begin applying these principles today, I can assure you that you will look upon this year as the greatest year of your life, because you have lived life as it was meant to be lived—in the freedom of constant forgiveness.

Have you ever heard of Wrong-way Roy? His actual name was Roy Riegels, and he played in the 1929 Rose Bowl. Roy was an All-America center for the University of California (Berkeley) Golden Bears, who were facing the Georgia Tech Yellowjackets. Roy played both offense and defense.

Toward the end of the first half, a Tech player fumbled the ball. Roy picked up the loose ball and started running furiously toward the goal some sixty-five yards away. There was only one problem—it was the wrong goal line! Fortunately, one of Roy's teammates, Benny Lom, took off in hot pursuit of Wrong-way Roy and tackled him just before he crossed the wrong goal line.

Halftime came, and you can imagine Roy's shame and embarrassment as he left the field, no doubt with head hanging low. He probably thought he was finished in that game and football in general. Everybody in the stadium was wondering what Nibbs Price, the California coach, would do with Roy Riegels.

As the team sat in the locker room, the coach remained quiet. The only sound was that of Roy Riegels, sitting in the corner and crying like a baby. Finally, the coach stood and announced to the team, "Men, the same team that started the first half will start the second half."

Roy Riegels lifted his head. His eyes were red, and his cheeks were wet with tears. "Coach, I can't do it. I've ruined you. I've ruined the University of California. I've ruined myself. I couldn't face that crowd in the stadium to save my life."

Coach Price reached out his hand and said, "Roy, get up and go on back; the game is only half over."

Riegels got up and went out to give one of the most inspiring individual efforts in Rose Bowl history.

So if you have fallen or stumbled in your spiritual walk, it's time to get up. Even if you've been going the wrong way up to this point in life, it's not too late to change your direction. The game is not over. There's a second chance waiting for you. You can experience the freedom of God's forgiveness—starting today.

NOTES

Chapter 2: The Seeking Shepherd

1. Chuck Smith, *Harvest* (Grand Rapids, Mich.: Fleming H. Revell, 1987).
2. W. Phillip Keller, *A Shepherd Looks at Psalm 23* (Grand Rapids, Mich.: Zondervan, 1996).
3. C. S. Lewis, *Surprised by Joy* (New York: Harcourt Brace, 1956).

Chapter 4: An Incomplete Surrender

1. A. W. Tozer, *That Incredible Christian* (Camp Hill, Pa.: Christian Publications, 1964).

Chapter 7: Second Chances for Shattered Lives

1. Greg Laurie, *The Great Compromise* (Dallas: Word Publishing, 1994), 109–29.

Chapter 10: A Second Chance to Follow God's Will

1. Charles H. Spurgeon, *The Quotable Spurgeon* (Wheaton, Ill.: Harold Shaw Publishers, 1990).

Chapter 12: A Second Chance after Tragedy

1. Warren Wiersbe and David Wiersbe, *Comforting the Bereaved* (Chicago: Moody Press, 1985).
2. Candy Lightner, *Giving Sorrow Words* (New York: Penguin Books, 1978).

Chapter 14: A Hunger for Home

1. A. W. Tozer, *Root of the Righteous* (Camp Hill, Pa.: Christian Publications, 1955, 1986).

Chapter 17: The Freedom of Forgiveness

1. I am indebted to the late Martin Lloyd-Jones for his excellent outline of 2 Peter. See his *Expository Sermons on 2 Peter* (Edinburgh, Scotland: The Banner of Truth, n.d.).

THE GOD
OF THE
SECOND
ChANCE

GReG Laurie

TYNDALE HOUSE PUBLISHERS, INC., WHEATON, ILLINOIS

Library of Congress Cataloging-in-Publication Data

Laurie, Greg.
  The God of the second chance : experiencing forgiveness / Greg Laurie.
    p. cm.
Originally published: Dallas : Word Pub., c1997.
Includes bibliographical references.
ISBN 0-8423-5582-0 (pbk.)
1. Forgiveness—Religious aspects—Christianity.   2. Forgiveness of sin.   3. Guilt—Religious aspects—Christianity.   4. Christian life.   I. Title.
BV4647.F55 L38 2002
234'.5—dc21   2001006273

Printed in the United States of America

07 06 05 04 03 02
7   8   6   5   4   3   2   1